TEACHING STUDENTS TO THINK

Dr. John Langrehr

Senior Lecturer in Education
South Australian College of Education

TEACHER'S MANUAL

NATIONAL EDUCATIONAL SERVICE

Bloomington, IN 1988

Editor: Dr. Jay McTighe
Education Specialist
Thinking Improvement Program
Maryland State Department of Education

Assistant Editor: Faridah Pawan
Indiana University, Bloomington, Indiana

Cover Design by Charles Neumeyer

Printed in the United States of America

Teaching Students to Think

INTRODUCTION

Jay McTighe, *editor*

The 19th century sculptor, Rodin, offers an insight into the nature of thinking through his famous bronze statue, *The Thinker*. The "thinker" is rendered in a seated, contemplative pose with the right elbow resting on the left knee and the chin supported by the back of the right hand. A close examination of this pose, or a brief assumption of this posture, will reveal that this is not a natural or comfortable position! Indeed, Rodin's sculpture can serve as a symbol to all eduators interested in improving the quality of the thinking of their student by reminding us that good thinking may not be a natural act. Effective critical and creative thinking demands effort, may be uncomfortable at times, and requires opportunities for deliberate reflection.

Fortunately for educators, research from various fields, including philosophy, cognititve psychology, linguistics, artificial intelligence, and brain research, contributes to our understanding of thinking and its development. We have learned, for instance, that sophisticated thinking does not develop automatically as a by-product of other instructional activities. Simply asking "higher level" questions does not ensure that students have the necessary knowledge or thinking abilities to answer them. Merely holding a classroom debate does not teach students how to structure an effective argument or assume a devil's advocate position. Likewise, the assignment of a writing or a problem-solving task does not, by itself, explicate the strategies used by successful writers of problem solvers. In each of these cases, a more explicit approach to the development of thinking is in order.

An explicit approach to the teaching of the development of thinking can be utilized within the classroom. For example, the use of terminology such as, *What do you **predict** will happen based on the pattern that we observed?; What underlying **assumptions** do you detect in the argument?; What evidence can you locate to support your **hypothesis**?*, reinforces the application of thinking skills in naturally occurring curriculum contexts. Another aspect of explicitness involves having students reflect on their own thinking processes. Teachers can promote student metacognition by taking time to discuss the thinking strategies involved in various academic tasks. They can also help to make the invisible process of thinking more tangible to students by "thinking aloud" to reveal their own reasoning processes.

Studies of transfer point out that most students do not spontaneously apply the thinking skills learned in one situation to new contexts. However, teachers can facilitate transfer by seeking opportunities to help students explore the application of specific thinking skills in many contexts within their own subject area, in other subjects, and outside of school.

Since good thinking is more than just skillful thinking, teachers can include discussions of the qualities of effective thinkers, such as *flexibility, openmindedness, reflection,* and *willingness to seek other points of view*. In addition to rewarding the display of such dispositions by their students, teachers can model these habits and attitudes of good thinking through their daily activities and interactions.

Finally, the explicit approach to developing thinking includes the **direct** teaching of thinking skills and processes when necessary and appropriate. It is within this context that the book, *Teaching Students To Think*, provides a valuable resource by offering teachers a volume of practical exercises for introducing and reinforcing a variety of fundamental thinking skills. Each exercise allows teachers and students to focus on a selected thinking skill while serving as a stimulant for thoughtful discussion, a springboard to metacognition, and a base from which to "bridge" thinking into various curriculum areas.

It has been noted that the greatest natural resource for the Information Ages lies in the capacity of the human mind for critical and creative thinking. Although the goal of developing thinking abilities through education is certainly not new, its realization has never been more important. The following proverb, of ancient origins, offers relevant wisdom for today's educators interested in the full development of mental potential:

"Give a man a fish and he will eat today.
Teach him to fish and he'll eat for a lifetime."

PREFACE

Large national and international studies such as the National Assessment of Educational Progress have revealed a "mindlessness" about the way in which many students think about curriculum content. Facts and processes are often rote learned and stored in the brain as isolated pieces of information. A program of thinking skills exercises can promote more mindful processing of information to help it become more meaningful and lasting.

This book provides exercises for students to practice most of the twenty core thinking skills identified by the American Association for Supervision and Curriculum Development (ASCD), in its publication *Dimensions of Thinking* (1987). These skills are practiced using content from mathematics and language, social studies, and science. This curriculum content should help students see the relevance of thinking skills when thinking about the content of any subject. It should also enable teachers to check whether students have made meaningful and creative links between the key concepts from these curriculum areas during their first six to eight years of schooling.

No special teacher training or workshops are needed to use these exercises. Both teachers and students can learn as they go through the exercises. The main requirement is a non-threatening, co-operative classroom atmosphere in which everyone is prepared to learn new ways of thinking about curriculum content.

To Dr. Jack R. Frymier, Senior Fellow at Phi Delta Kappa, the most creative and inspirational educator I ever met.

CONTENTS

PAGE

INTRODUCTION by Jay McTighe (i)
TO THE LEARNER (ii)

INFORMATION GATHERING & ORGANIZING SKILLS

1	Observing Things Carefully	2-3
2	Comparing Similar Properties of Things	4-6
3	Comparing Different Properties of Things	7-9
4	Classifying Things into Categories 1	10-12
5	Classifying Things into Categories 2	13-16
6	Classifying Things into Categories 3	17-21
7	Identifying the Essential Properties of a Concept	22-24
8	Ordering Concepts in Terms of Size	25-27
9	Ordering Concepts in Terms of Time	28-29

ANALYZING SKILLS

10	Identifying Relationships	31-32
11	Identifying Patterns in Sequences	33-34
12	Identifying Patterns in Figure—Letter— Number Sequences	35-36
13	Identifying Extreme Properties of Something 1	37-38
14	Identifying Extreme Properties of Something 2	39-41
15	Thinking About Creative Structures	42

GENERATING SKILLS

16	Representing Related Concepts	44-47
17	Representing Things with Shared Properties	48-52
18	Elaborating Meaning to New Words	53-55
19	Representing the Meaning of Instructions	56-58
20	Representing "No, All, Some" Statements	59-62
21	Making Inferences From Observations	63-65
22	Making Inferences From Advertisements	66-68
23	Generalizing	69-73
24	Thinking Flexibly About Problems	74-75
25	Defining Mathematics Problems with Sketches	76-80

EVALUATING SKILLS

26	Identifying Errors 1 — Facts From Opinions	82-83
27	Identifying Errors 2 — Poor Reasoning	84-85
28	Identifying Errors 3 — Relevance of Information	86-87
29	Establishing Criteria for Decision Making 1	88-89
30	Establishing Criteria for Decision Making 2	90-94
31	Establishing Criteria for Finding a Cause	95-99
32	Verifying the Accuracy of Someone's Claim	100-102
33	Identifying Errors 4 — Misleading Statements	103-104

INTEGRATING SKILLS

34	Summarizing A Reading	106-109

TO THE LEARNER

Flexible thinking is not memorizing correct answers for a test. Flexible thinking is being able to think **about different ways** of solving a problem, of making a decision, of looking at something, in new ways.

When you leave school you will have to make decisions and solve problems every day. These two important thinking processes will be used in your work. They will also be used when you buy, select, build, repair, and play something away from work.

It is important to remember as much information as you can. This saves the time looking it up in a book or from a computer. However, you must also learn to make flexible or creative links between information. Only you can learn to do this by observing and thinking about things in a completely different way.

The exercises in this book will help you to "free up" your mind. Many of the questions have more than one correct answer. Feel free to come up with different, but possible answers. However, be prepared to defend or explain your answers to those who think they are not suitable. Listen to the answers of other people and to how they came up with these answers.

Critical thinking is more than criticizing what other people write and say.

When we think critically we should be aware of particular aspects of the information we are criticizing. We should also try to put ourselves in the other person's position and see the reason for his or her argument or statement.

Some aspects of a statement that we can criticize include:

1)   the truth of the statement;
2)   the relevance of the statement;
3)   the accuracy of the statement and
4)   any bias and inconsistency in the statement.

The groups of exercises on critical thinking aim to help you become a fair-minded person and a person who thinks about information before blindly accepting it.

Politicians and business leaders make decisions that affect us every day. Journalists report articles in the newspaper for us to read each day. And advertisers try to tempt us each day with eye-catching statements on TV, the newspaper and magazines.

We should all have the skill to think carefully and critically about these decisions, articles and advertisements. Don't depend on other people to tell you what is good or bad, a fact or an opinion, a biased or unbiased statement and so on.

Flexible and critical thinking are skills that, once developed, will benefit you for the rest of your life.

Good thinking!

JOHN LANGREHR, Ph.D
Senior Lecturer
South Australian C.A.E.,
Holbrooks Road,
Underdale,
South Australia, 5032

SOME THOUGHTS FOR TEACHERS

1. WHY TEACH THINKING SKILLS?

How are ice, wood, and oil similar?
What are the essential features for a one cent coin?
What are five quite different uses for a one cent coin?
What are some possible causes for your bedroom light not working when you turn it on?
What does an advertisement that says "Buy your home, only minutes from the city" really mean?

You may never have thought about these questions before. And yet, somewhere in your brain you have made quite unusual and even unplanned connections between components of this incoming information. The questions here act as a stimulus to activate these connections and consequently help you come up with some answers. Somehow we all develop thinking skills to varying degrees. These skills help us make useful and creative connections between incoming information and information previously stored in our brain.

In order to answer the first of the five questions above, we use the skill of **categorizing**. Most of us have categorized ice, wood and oil as being things that float, or that occur naturally, or that contain hydrogen. The second question involves us using the skill of **generalizing**. The third question involves us **analyzing** attributes and thinking **flexibly** about them. The last question involves us making **inferences** based on various associated assumptions. Categorizing, generalizing, **analyzing** attributes, and making **inferences** represent only four of the twenty core thinking skills identified by the Association for Supervision and Curriculum Development in their publication *Dimensions of Thinking*[1]. (See Figure 1).

You may have noticed that each of the above questions have more than one correct answer. In this sense the questions are quite different from those asked in most school and college courses, where each question generally has only one correct answer. And yet, the multi-answer questions here are the kinds of questions that we have to face up to in problem solving and in decision making — the most common, daily thinking activities in 'life after school.' Of course, much of the content we have been forced to memorize at school is useful in these activities. However, unless we have developed strategies or skills for making imaginative and untaught connections between this content and the goal at hand, we will be limited in the kinds of solutions we come up within our future problem solving and decision making.

---

1. *Dimensions of Thinking,* ASCD, Virginia, 1987.

FIGURE 1
Core Thinking Skills from ASCD's Dimensions of Thinking

Core Thinking Skills.
Thinking skills are relatively discrete cognitive operations that can be considered the "building blocks" of thinking. The following skills (1) have a sound basis in the research and theoretical literature, (2) are important for students to be able to do, and (3) can be taught and be reinforced in school.

Focusing skills — directing one's attention to selected information.
 1. Defining problems — clarifying problem situations.
 2. Setting goals — establishing direction and purpose.

Information gathering skills — acquiring relevant data.
 3. Observing — obtaining information through one or more senses.
 4. Questioning — seeking new information by formulating questions.

Remembering skills — storing and retrieving information.
 5. Encoding — storing information in long-term memory.
 6. Recalling — retrieving information from long-term memory.

Organizing skills — arranging information so it can be used more effectively.
 7. Comparing — noting similarities and differences between two or more entities.
 8. Classifying — placing entities in groups by common attributes.
 9. Ordering — sequencing entities according to a given criterion.

Analyzing skills — clarifying existing information by identifying and distinguishing among components, attributes, and so on.
 10. Identifying attributes and components — determining characteristics or parts of something.
 11. Identifying relationships and patterns — recognizing ways elements are related.

Generating skills — using prior knowledge to add new information.
 12. Inferring — reasoning beyond available information to fill in gaps.
 13. Predicting — anticipating or forecasting future events.
 14. Elaborating — using prior knowledge to add meaning to new information and to link it to existing structures.
 15. Representing — adding new meaning by changing the form of information.

Integrating skills — connecting and combining information.
 16. Summarizing — abstracting information efficiently and parsimoniously.
 17. Restructuring — changing existing knowledge structures to incorporate new information.

Evaluating skills — assessing the reasonableness and quality of ideas.
 18. Establishing criteria — setting standards for making judgments.
 19. Verifying — confirming the accuracy of claims.
 20. Identifying errors — recognizing logical fallacies.

It is too much of a risk to assume that all students will quite naturally develop the wide range of core thinking skills identified by ASCD.

It is also too much of a risk to assume that all teachers know what these skills are and can model them through expert questioning in all subjects of the curriculum. There is a need for courses that identify a range of thinking skills for both teachers and students. An aim of such courses would be to improve the kinds of questions that both teachers and students ask themselves and each other about content that they may have been happy to just memorize in the past.

Perhaps the most powerful argument for teaching thinking skills through a series of exercises like those in this book is that they "free up" student thinking. Thinking skills exercises provide a balance in the curriculum to the convergent, one correct answer type thinking emphasized in the traditional subjects. Much of a student's time in studying these subjects is spent on memorizing the one correct answer for each of a multitude of questions and problems. It is fairly easy to test and objectively assess whether a student has or has not correctly memorized such answers. Then it is easy to award a grade for comparing the achievement of students.

An unfortunate by-product of such a traditional, but necessary process is the blunting of the flexibility and inquisitiveness of student thinking. You only have to compare the number of "Why?" and "How?" questions of young, wide-eyed students starting school with those of much older students to confirm this claim. And yet, as already suggested, on leaving school students need all of the flexibility of thought they can muster. As the world shrinks and systems become more automated, the development, and in some cases, the survival, of an individual, a town, or a nation depends on the ability to respond to change. Specialized courses that identify and allow the practice of thinking skills, followed by their infusion across the curriculum have an important part to play in preparing individuals to meet this challenge.

2. WHO ARE THE EXERCISES FOR?

It is suggested that the exercises in this book are suitable for students in grade 6 through 9. However, even adults will have fun and be challenged by the thinking skills exercises.

The exercises should be most useful for —

1) grade 6/8 students taking a weekly lesson on thinking skills as part of a math, language, or social education program.

2) grade 8/9 remedial or English as a second language students. Many of the exercises are language oriented. They require students to think about the meaning of concepts, the relationships between them and so on.

3) grade 4/5 gifted students. The open-ended nature of many of the exercises will allow these students to share with each other creative connections between concepts and creative solutions in problem solving and other thinking activities.

3. WHAT ARE THE EXERCISES ABOUT?

The exercises in this book aim to provide examples for most of the core thinking skills identified by ASCD. The sequencing of the exercises takes into account the developmental process of acquiring thinking skills. The early exercises involve observing, comparing, categorizing, ordering and identifying attributes, relationships and patterns. The latter exercises include inferring, representing, summarizing, establishing criteria, verifying, and identifying errors.

Perhaps the most under-estimated and poorly developed thinking skills in learners are those of the **Observing** and the **Questioning** of characteristics of the things they observe. This is summed up in a personal verse —

> *We see trees, but not the shape of their leaves.*
> *We see wood, but not the patterns in its grain.*
> *We see friends, but not the color of their eyes.*
>
> *How much of our world do we really see each day?*

The first exercise in the book tries to get students to think about their previous observations of common things about them. It aims to help students realize that different people can see quite different features in a common object. For example, a key for some students is nothing more than something used to open a door. Other students may see a key as being metallic, magnetic, smooth on one edge and crinkled on the other, holed in one end, and identified with a number and brand name. And still a few others may see a key as a symbol of freedom or of attaining adulthood.

The exercise is meant to indicate to students that people have quite different thoughts about common experiences. It also announces that thinking skills exercises are in general non-threatening because of the opportunity they offer for coming up with a variety of possible answers depending on one's past experience and special interests.

The 'things' provided in many of the exercises as a stimulus for thinking about generally start with concrete, everyday objects containing few parts. Then more abstract, observable things such as geometric shapes, numbers and words are included. Finally, key concepts from the various subjects of the curriculum are used. For example, in one exercise students are asked to think about the characteristics of a flag, then the number 6 or a black, geometric shape, and later on, an island, a planet, and a law.

After the initial exercise on observing, various **organizing** skills for arranging incoming information are modelled. These skills include **comparing** or noting similarities and differences between things, **classifying** or placing things into groups based on common characteristics, and **ordering** things in a sequence depending on changing patterns or a characteristic.

Analyzing skills follow these organizing skills. Exercises that help students **identify** common and essential attributes of given things and also identify **relationships** between pairs and sequences of things are provided.

Many of the difficulties of student thinking result from their inability to accurately image abstract information in their minds. The **generating skills** of **elaborating** and **representing** information aim to help imaging. Representing related concepts through concept mapping, family trees, and "no, all or some" diagrams, and shared property maps are some of the exercises here. The needs to clearly represent given data with diagrams, tables, graphs and so on, is referred to again in a later sequence of exercises on problem solving. Elaborating "meaning" to unknown words and to given instructions are other exercises that help students to generate or use prior knowledge to add new information.

Inferring, another important generating skill is the focus of two more exercises. Students are encouraged to think carefully about the conclusions they draw from statements they read or hear, particularly in advertisements, and from observations they make each day. The assumptions that accompany such inferences is made clear.

One cluster of exercises involve what *Dimensions of Thinking* identifies as being **integrating** and **evaluating** skills. For example, helping students to **identify errors** in statements of facts and opinions, in poor reasoning, and in relevant and irrelevant information occupies three exercises. The skill of **verifying** the accuracy of the claims of other people is also introduced. Three exercises on the skill of **establishing criteria** for making judgements are provided. These involve making decisions that affect oneself and those that affect other people. One exercise helps students develop criteria for thinking about the **cause** for a particular observation made.

This cluster of **evaluating skills** are part of what has been termed **critical thinking**. The earlier exercises in the book focus more on **analytical thinking**. There is also a small group of exercises that are concerned with **creative thinking**. These include a consideration of creative structures and the inventions of other people. Together, they aim to encourage more flexible and creative thinking.

4. HOW CAN YOU USE THE EXERCISES IN CLASS?

There are several principles to keep in mind when working through any thinking skills exercise.

4.1 At the end of an exercise it is important that all students be given the opportunity to talk 'out loud' the thoughts they had in coming up with a particular answer. The sharing of thoughts, particularly of good thinkers with less able thinkers, is a critical part of all thinking courses. Remember that thinking skills exercises only provide a stimulus for practicing a particular skill. The free discussion, debate, and defense of particular opinions and solutions is where students really learn to change their usual and perhaps limited ways of thinking about things.

A knowledge of correct answers does little to improve the thinking of students. It is the knowledge of the thinking processes used to come up with these answers that is important.

4.2 The sequencing of items within an exercise

In any lesson it is always a good idea to proceed from the known to the unknown, from the simple to the complex, and from the concrete to the abstract. Consequently, encourage students to follow the items in the order they are given in each exercise. However, it is also a good idea to allow students to start off with some items that refer to a particular interest such as a sport, or a hobby.

4.3 The establishment of a non-threatening environment

As previously mentioned, it is important to establish a non-threatening environment and cooperative classroom environment. Don't be quick to judge a student's answer that may at first appear inappropriate. Encourage even the most introverted student to offer an answer. Often these students have a special interest, hobby, or skill that enables them to come up with a rather unique answer or opinion. Be prepared to show your own difficulty in coming up with an answer to a particular item. Less able students will be encouraged by this honesty and sense that even adults can be challenged by thinking skills exercises.

4.4 A discussion of the application of a thinking skill

It is important for students to see some relevance or application for a particular thinking skill modelled in an exercise. Consequently, after introducing a skill through the example provided in an exercise, a class generated list of applications in other subjects of the curriculum should be recorded on blackboard or chart paper.

Consider Exercise 2. "Comparing Similar Properties of Things." After listening to the example, and asking questions about it, the class might suggest the following applications —

the similarity between two or more
— specimens or animals in science
— characters in a play or story
— geometric figures
— wars
— political systems, countries, games, chemicals, processes, paintings, periods of history, materials, techniques and so on.

This kind of warm-up activity highlights the transfer of the skill to other subjects. It helps motivate students. A discussion of the answers to a few of these student examples can help slower thinking students by reinforcing the kind of thinking needed to answer the items in the exercise.

4.5 **The need for feedback on completing an exercise**

A hurried five minute announcement of possible answers for items at the end of a lesson will do little to change the way students think. It is better to stop students after ten or fifteen minutes of work and then have some students talk through their thinking for various items.

When, fast working students have completed an exercise it is a good idea to have them create their own items. These can be modelled on those completed in the exercise. An "item bank" of such student generated items could be useful for class checkout quizzes.

5. **APPLYING THINKING SKILLS ACROSS THE CURRICULUM**

5.1 Like all skills, thinking skills need to be continually used if they are to be retained and refined.

The classroom teacher should always be on the lookout for opportunities to apply particular thinking skills to appropriate content in their courses.

For example, in a math lesson don't give up the opportunity of **comparing** or **categorizing** geometric shapes. In a science lesson ask students to **generalize** about the characteristics of particular groups of specimens. In a history lesson point out the **inference and assumptions** made in an historical account of any event. In a technical studies or craft lesson occasionally stop to **analyze the invention** of some past inventor in terms of its parts, its shape, the material it is made of, and how it has been improved. In a consumer education lesson, use a newspaper to critically analyze the **hidden meaning** of an advertisement, the **relevance** of some information, the **bias** in a report or cartoon, and the **accuracy** of someone's claim about something they have observed.

In all of the above activities the teacher is **infusing** the particular thinking skill into subject matter from a course in the curriculum. This is the ideal. Each time we stop to refer to a particular thinking skill in this way, the skill comes into sharp focus. It's relevance to real world issues is reinforced and the vocabulary and processes associated with the skill are more likely to become a natural part of a student's future thinking.

In order to identify opportunities for infusing thinking skills into curriculum content, passages within text books or other teaching resources can be annotated by the teacher. For example, a page mentioning different kinds of animals, occupations, food, clothing, sports and so on could be marked "Categorizing." Another page giving someone's description of a current or historical event could be marked "Bias/Accuracy."

A homework reading with many related concepts could be marked "Concept Mapping," which suggests that students could summarize the reading with a visual display of a hierarchy of concepts linked by connecting terms.

All teachers should see themselves as teachers of thinking rather than as 'content sprayers.' The annotation of text books and other teaching resources in this way is a way of getting involved. It could be a good idea to work through a subject matter text book with a checklist similar to the one shown here.

ANNOTATING TEACHING RESOURCES FOR APPLYING THINKING SKILLS

1. Comparing — At least two things with quite similar or quite different properties are presented for comparison.

2. Categorizing — A variety of similar things are presented that can be placed into categories based on common features.

3. Analyzing — Things with a variety of parts, shapes, uses, patterns, styles, relationships — are available for analysis.

4. Generalizing — A variety of data or examples is given for a common thing from which generalizations can be made.

5. Representing — Verbal information or a problem is provided that can easily be represented as a sketch, graph, table, etc.

   — Verbal information containing many related concepts is available for concept mapping.

6. Evaluating — Statements or reports by individuals are available that can be evaluated in terms of bias, relevance, accuracy of claim, and truth.

7. Inferring — Observations or statements are available for allowing possible conclusions to be made.

5.2 The statements, instructions, and questions of teachers themselves can also help develop the thinking of their students. Communications such as these can either involve little or much inferencing, searching for meaning and so on by each student. If students are continually spoon fed with closed, definite communications then they have to do minimal thinking. The teacher has already done it for them. The teacher who asks more searching and open "Why?" and "How?" questions forces students to mentally manipulate associated information rather than to passively soak it up.

It is important for teachers to continue to use the thinking skills terminology of the exercise in this book in future classroom communications. For example, questions can begin with —

1) *What **evidence** do you have for...?*
2) *What **criteria** do you use to...?*
3) *How can we **classify**...?*
4) ***Predict** the feeding habits of this bird...?*
5) *How do you **compare** these two substances...?*
6) *What can we **infer** from this advertisement...?*

These and similar key terms should be on the "tips of the tongues" of students as they think about things they read, see and hear. Every subject of the curriculum has its own terminology. For example, to a chemistry student, a substance may be crystalline, amorphous, an element, a metalloid and so on. Students who understand and use such terms regularly observe and think about substances in a completely different way from those who have not studied chemistry.

And so it is with the terminology of thinking. Those students who understand and use the terms regularly have different mental spring boards for observing and thinking about future information they are confronted with.

Teachers can also help the development of their students' thinking by challenging any generalizations or vague language used in student statements. For example —

1) when a student states that **everybody** or something **always** happens, the teacher should ask for specific examples.

2) when a student states that something is **better**, **cheaper** and so on, the teacher should ask for what it is being compared with.

3) when a student states that **they, this group of things,** or a similar undefined group acts in a certain way the teacher should ask for specific cases or names.

A set of exercises on a wide range of core thinking skills is only a start for improving the thinking of students. If taught as an isolated set of intelligence test items and then never referred to again, their value would be lost. The continued reference to the principles, processes and terminology learned in thinking skills exercises is essential. Annotating teaching resources, using better teacher "Why?" and "How?" questions, challenging vague student generalizations, and continually using the terminology of thinking skills are some easy ways of infusing thinking skills across the curriculum.

5.3 Students themselves have a part to play in infusing thinking skills across the curriculum. They too should be on the look out for content that lends itself to a particular skill. Some of the exercises in this book have spaces at the end for student examples. After completing an exercise students should be encouraged to think up one or two items that model the skill using content from their science, social studies, language, math, and creative performing arts courses. These items could be developed for homework and shared with the class. In this way an item bank of questions in science, social studies and so on that model a particular thinking skill can be developed.

6. HOW DO YOU ASSESS THINKING SKILLS?

Different people will **see** different properties in a common object. They will think of various ways in which it is **similar** to another object. They will use different **categories** for placing the object into. For many of the core thinking skills such as observing, comparing, and categorizing, there are different, and yet correct, ways of thinking about a given stimuli or question. The beauty of many of the items in this book is that they have a "band of correct answers" rather than a single, correct answer. The items are mind expanding rather than mind contracting. They encourage the development of new and creative links between concepts already stored in the brain.

For any multiple answer item or question some students may come up with only one or two of these answers. Other students will generate many more. No one is right or wrong. However, some students are thinking more fluently and flexibly than others. The question is "How do we give a mark or grade to the students for their answers?" We could total the number of possible answers given by a student for all items in a test. Alternatively, we could give an A for a range of total possible answers, a B for another range and so on.

Obviously, the assessment of most thinking skills cannot be as objective as the assessement of content that has only one correct answer. However, the aim of tests of thinking skills should not be to compare students, but rather to indicate personal improvement by individual students.

The assessment of thinking skills is a problem still under investigation by many researchers. There are no easy answers to the problem. Any thoughts of using 'one correct answer' type tests, followed by grading to compare students, would appear to go against a major aim of thinking skills programs — that is to think more flexibly.

7. A FINAL WORD

If we haven't taught students how to think creatively and carefully by the time they start senior high school, then it is almost too late. We have wasted a wonderful opportunity in a period of learning where the student is still excited by learning.

Learning the skill of thinking can be both challenging and fun. Once learned, these skills can be used in all kinds of situations throughout one's life. Decision making and solving personal problems and work related problems are major thinking activities of adulthood.

When students have completed these exercises and have understood the skills involved, they will hopefully start to observe and think about their world in a completely different way.

JOHN LANGREHR
South Australian College of Advanced Education,
Adelaide,
South Australia.

INFORMATION GATHERING
AND
ORGANIZING SKILLS

Exercises 1-9 aim to help you gain and arrange information so that it can be used more effectively.

The skills include —

Observing —   obtaining information through looking.

Comparing —   noting similarities and differences.

Classifying —   placing things into groups by common properties.

Ordering —   sequencing things in a pattern or in a prescribed way.

1.   OBSERVING THINGS CAREFULLY

Good thinkers are good observers. Good thinkers are also good at asking themselves questions about the things that they observe.

Tree trunks are **round**.   Why?
Stop signs are **red**.   Why?
Pencils are made of **wood**.   Why?
Fish have **scales**.   Why?

Most things about us have special properties or features that we can observe if we really look carefully. For example, they have —

Shape	Uses	Parts
Color	Materials	Size

The first letters of these six properties form the word **SCUMPS**. Remember this one word and you can remember **six** common properties of things.

Things made by nature or things made by humans usually have their particular shape, color and other properties for a special reason. Start asking yourself questions about these reasons and you will start seeing your world in a completely different way.

WRITE DOWN *AT LEAST FOUR PROPERTIES* YOU OBSERVE FOR EACH OF THE FOLLOWING THINGS. I HOPE YOU CAN FIND MORE. USE THE WORD SCUMPS TO HELP YOU. **WRITE DOWN A REASON** WHY THE OBJECT HAS EACH PROPERTY THAT YOU LIST.

THINGS	PROPERTIES	REASONS FOR PROPERTY
1. A BRICK	• HARD • ROUGH • HEAVY	• WON'T CHIP OR WEAR • CEMENT STICKS STRONGLY • WALL WON'T TOPPLE OVER EASILY • EASILY STACK ON TOP OF EACH OTHER IN WALLS.
2. A COIN	• ROUND • METALLIC • THIN • FACE ON FRONT	• EASY TO HANDLE/STORE • WON'T BEND EASILY • LIGHT • COUNTRY'S HISTORY

THINGS	PROPERTIES	REASONS FOR PROPERTY
3. A FLAG	• COLORED • PATTERNED • MADE OF CLOTH • RECTANGULAR	• EASY TO SEE • REPRESENTS PEOPLE • DIFFICULT TO TEAR • EASY TO MAKE
4. A TREE	• HAS LEAVES • HAS ROOTS • ROUND TRUNK • UPRIGHT	• TO TAKE IN GASES • TO KEEP TREE STABLE • STRENGTH • TO REACH FOR SUNLIGHT
5. A PENCIL	• WOODEN • SIX SIDED • CARBON LEAD • THIN	• EASY TO SHARPEN • EASY TO HOLD/STORE • MARKS EASILY • EASY TO HOLD
6. A CAR TIRE	• ROUND • MADE OF RUBBER • HOLLOW • GROOVED	• SMOOTH TO ROLL • FLEXIBLE • FOR FLEXING • GRIP ON ROAD

2.   COMPARING SIMILAR PROPERTIES OF THINGS

The first exercise aimed to help you think more flexibly and carefully about the properties of one thing at a time.

This exercise aims to help you think more flexibly about two things at a time.

Two things may at first look quite different. However, if we look a little closer, and think about what we see, the things are sure to have some properties that are the same. Comparing things in this way will help you store similar things in your brain for future use.

WRITE DOWN *AT LEAST THREE WAYS* IN WHICH THE FOLLOWING PAIRS OF THINGS ARE THE SAME.
USE THE WORD **"SCUMPS"** TO HELP YOU.
WHEN YOU HAVE FINISHED, COMBINE ALL THE DIFFERENT ANSWERS FROM OTHER STUDENTS.

TWO THINGS	SIMILAR PROPERTIES
1. a RAKE and a COMB	HAVE PRONGS, MACHINE MADE, KEEP THINGS TIDY
2. a BANANA and a LEMON	HAVE THICK SKIN, ARE FRUIT, GROWN ON A TREE, ARE FOOD

TWO THINGS	SIMILAR PROPERTIES

3. a TENNIS BALL

and

a MARBLE

ARE ROUND, USED IN GAMES,
MACHINE MADE, BOUNCE

4. a SQUARE

and

a TRIANGLE

HAVE SIDES, HAVE ANGLES, ARE CLOSED
FIGURES, ARE TWO-DIMENSIONAL

5. an ANT

and

a PINE TREE

BOTH LIVING, NEED WATER, NEED AIR,
NEED SUN, HAVE BODY SYSTEMS

PAIRS OF THINGS	SIMILAR PROPERTIES

Here are some things from **Mathematics and Language Arts**.

6.	the NUMBERS 2 and 6	BOTH EVEN, SINGLE DIGITS, DIVIDE INTO 12
7.	the NUMBERS 4 and 9	BOTH SINGLE DIGITS, HAVE EXACT SQUARE ROOTS, DIVIDE INTO 36
8.	a SQUARE a CIRCLE	CLOSED FIGURES, 2 DIMENSIONAL, GEOMETRIC SHAPES
9.	the WORDS FELL, RAN	ARE VERBS, HAVE ONE VOWEL, ARE PAST TENSE, CONTAIN CAPITAL LETTERS

Here are some things from **Science**.

10.	a VEIN a GARDEN HOSE	CARRY LIQUIDS, THIN WALLED, HOLLOW, BEND EASILY
11.	a FROG a SEAL	ANIMALS, LIVE IN AND OUT OF WATER, HAVE BONES, BLOOD, BODY SYSTEMS

Here are some things from **Social Studies**.

12.	a FAMILY a TEAM	A GROUP OF PEOPLE, HAVE A NAME, HAVE A LEADER, HAVE RULES
13.	a PRESIDENT a PRIME MINISTER	ELECTED, HEADS OF COUNTRIES, POLITICIANS

Now try to make up some of your own examples from mathematics, science and social studies. Write in some possible answers for your exercises.

3.   COMPARING DIFFERENT PROPERTIES OF THINGS

Differences between things are also interesting and useful to us for sorting these things into groups or categories.

Sometimes a difference can be very important in giving something an **advantage** over something else.

WRITE DOWN **AT LEAST THREE WAYS** IN WHICH THE FIRST THING IS DIFFERENT FROM THE SECOND THING IN THE FOLLOWING PAIRS. THINK ABOUT ANY SPECIAL ADVANTAGE A DIFFERENCE GIVES THE FIRST THING OVER THE SECOND THING IN EACH PAIR. MENTION YOUR ADVANTAGES DURING CLASS DISCUSSION OF THE ITEMS.

THINGS	DIFFERENT PROPERTIES
1. a CAT and a DOG	CAN CLIMB TREES, CAN'T BARK, HAS FUR, LOW INTELLIGENCE
2. a CRAB and a FISH	HAS CLAWS, HARD SHELL, SWIMS BACKWARDS, CAN LIVE OUT OF WATER

THINGS	DIFFERENT PROPERTIES

3. an ANIMAL

and

a TREE

CAN MOVE ALONG GROUND,
HAS EYES, BLOOD, HAIR

4. a BICYCLE

and

a HORSE

MACHINE MADE, DOESN'T NEED FOOD,
LONG LIFE, STORE INSIDE HOUSE

5. a NEWSPAPER

and

a BOOK

LOW COST, PRINTED DAILY,
MANY WRITERS, CURRENT NEWS

6. an APPLE

and

a POTATO

A FRUIT, GROWS ON A TREE,
SEEDS INSIDE

Here are some things from **Mathematics and Language Arts**.

| 7. | a TRIANGLE | HAS STRAIGHT SIDES, ANGLES, VERTICES |
| | a CIRCLE | |

| 8. | the NUMBERS | IS EVEN, NOT A PRIME NUMBER, |
| | 4 and 11 | ONLY ONE DIGIT |

| 9. | the NUMBERS | IS ODD, EXACT SQUARE ROOT, |
| | 25 and 26 | DIVIDE BY FIVE |

| 10. | VERBS | SHOW ACTION, HAVE TENSES, FEWER |
| | NOUNS | IN NUMBER THAN NOUNS |

Here are some things from **Science**.

| 11. | a FROG | HAS LEGS, LUNGS, |
| | a TADPOLE | CAN LIVE OUT OF WATER |

| 12. | a BIRD | HAS 2 LEGS, BLOOD, BONES, |
| | a BEE | A LONGER LIFE SPAN |

| 13. | a LAKE | CAN BE FRESH WATER, SURROUNDED |
| | an OCEAN | BY LAND, SMALL TIDES |

| 14. | a VEIN | THIN WALLS, CARRIES BLOOD |
| | an ARTERY | TO HEART, MORE OF THEM |

Here are some things from **Social Studies**.

| 15. | a PRESIDENT | HEAD OF GOVERNMENT, |
| | a QUEEN | IS ELECTED, CAN BE A MAN |

| 16. | a DEMOCRACY | HAS LEADERS ELECTED BY THE PEOPLE, |
| | a DICTATORSHIP | HAS FREEDOM OF SPEECH |

4. CLASSIFYING THINGS INTO CATEGORIES I

The first three exercises have helped us observe and compare the properties of some things about us. Some of these things were living, some were machine made and some were symbols and diagrams that we humans use to store and develop knowledge.

Rather than memorizing the properties of all of the thousands of things we have observed in our lives, we cleverly remember the properties of the CATEGORIES we place these things into. For example, we remember the properties of animals, of metals, of clothes, of liquids, of insects and so on. If someone asks us to describe what iron is like, we first think about the properties of METALS, the category we have put iron into. Iron must therefore be hard, it must sink in water, it must get hot quickly, it must allow electricity to pass through it and so on. Other metals such as copper and titanium must also have these properties.

The more categories you can form in your brain and the more things you can place into these categories, the more CREATIVE or FLEXIBLE is your thinking.

THE FOLLOWING SETS OF THREE THINGS CAN BE PLACED INTO A COMMON CATEGORY. FIRST TRY TO FIND SOME SIMILAR PROPERTY BELONGING TO ALL THREE THINGS IN A SET. THEN WRITE DOWN THE NAME OF THE CATEGORY YOU CAN PLACE THEM INTO.

THINGS	CATEGORY USED
For example:	
apple, meat, cheese	FOOD

Now, here are some **common** things for you to categorize.

	THINGS	CATEGORY USED
1.	magnet, scissors, paper clip	MADE OF METAL
2.	pencil, book, tree	MADE OF WOOD
3.	hammer, brick, rock	HARD THINGS
4.	photograph, page, door	RECTANGULAR THINGS
5.	cork, iceberg, apple	FLOAT ON WATER
6.	tire, coin, cog	ROUND THINGS

10

THINGS	CATEGORY USED
7. fence, post, wall	VERTICAL THINGS

Here are some things from **Mathematics and Language Arts**.

THINGS	CATEGORY USED
8.	QUADRILATERALS
9. the numbers: 7, 11, 13	ODD/PRIME NUMBERS
10. the numbers: 16, 64, 36	PERFECT SQUARES
11. the numbers: 6, 15, 36	DIVISIBLE BY THREE
12. triangles, squares, pentagons	POLYGONS/CLOSED
13. the words: walk, catch, climb	VERBS
14. the words: you, she, this	PRONOUNS

Here are some things from **Science**.

THINGS	CATEGORY USED
15. beetle, ant, butterfly	INSECTS
16. heat, light, sound	FORMS OF ENERGY
17. rabbit, cow, deer	GRASS EATING ANIMALS
18. friction, gravity, push	FORCES
19. ice, steam, fog	FORMS OF WATER
20. glacier, wind, floods	CAUSE EROSION OF SOIL
21. dry cell, battery, generator	PRODUCE ELECTRICITY
22. fats, carbohydrates, protein	PARTS OF FOOD

THINGS	CATEGORY USED
23. uranium, coal, sunlight	CAN PRODUCE ELECTRICTY
24. jelly fish, coral, sponge	LIVE IN WATER
25. echo, thunder, music	SOUNDS
26. sulphur, oxygen, iron	CHEMICALS/ELEMENTS
27. koala, wombat, kangaroo	MARSUPIALS/ANIMALS
28. cotton, wool, hemp	NATURAL FIBERS
29. snake, alligator, lizard	REPTILES
30. lever, pulley, ramp	MAKE WORK EASIER
31. eye, telescope, camera	CONTAIN A LENS
32. photosynthesis, shadows, photoelectricity	REQUIRE LIGHT

Here are some things from **Social Studies**.

THINGS	CATEGORY USED
33. to eat, to drink, to sleep	HUMAN NEEDS
34. senator, election, vote	PARTS OF POLITICS

5. CLASSIFYING THINGS INTO CATEGORIES II

As we observe and learn more about things we get better and better pictures in our brains of the properties of things that belong to a category.

We also learn that some things can be placed into more than one category. For example **a car** could be placed in a category we call "things made of metal" or "things made by machine" or "things to travel in" and so on.

This exercise is a little more difficult in that the four things in each group could be placed in the same category. However, there is one thing in each group that does not have a property that the other three things have.

THE FOLLOWING LIST CONTAINS FOUR THINGS IN EACH SET. THREE OF THE THINGS CAN BE PLACED IN THE SAME CATEGORY.

WRITE DOWN THE THING THAT DOESN'T FIT INTO EACH CATEGORY. ALSO WRITE DOWN WHY IT DOESN'T BELONG THERE.

THINGS	DIFFERENT THING
For example:	
apple, carrot, banana, orange	CARROT (NOT A FRUIT)
Now, here are some **common** things	
1. car, truck, bicycle, bus	BICYCLE — NO MOTOR
2. cow, dog, horse, goat	DOG — EATS MEAT
3. monkey, dog, cat, squirrel	DOG — DOESN'T CLIMB TREES
4. red, green, blue, yellow	GREEN — NOT PRIMARY COLOR
5. hammer, drill, saw, plane	HAMMER — DOESN'T CUT
6. oranges, apples, lemons, grapefruits	APPLES — NOT CITRUS

THINGS	DIFFERENT THING
7. wood, rubber, plastic, cotton	PLASTIC — NOT NATURAL
8. rice, wheat, barley, sugar	SUGAR — NOT GRAIN CROP

Here are some things from **Mathematics and Language Arts**.

THINGS	DIFFERENT THING
9. the numbers: 12, 27, 25, 39	25 — NOT DIVISIBLE BY 3
10. 25, 16, 21, 36	21 — NO EXACT SQUARE ROOT
11. 0.75, 3/4, 75%, 75/1000	75/1000 NOT EQUAL TO .75
12.	NOT A PARALLELOGRAM
13. sphere, rectangle, cylinder, cube	RECTANGLE — NOT 3D
14.	NOT SYMMETRICAL
15. degrees, graph, seconds, grams	GRAPH — NOT A UNIT OF MEASUREMENT
16. went, smiles, climbed, sat	SMILES — NOT IN PAST TENSE
17. song, speech, mime, poetry	MIME — NO SPOKEN WORDS
18. parallelogram, rectangle, octagon, square	OCTAGON — NOT A 4 SIDED FIGURE
19. run, rag, rat, ram	RUN — NOT A NOUN
20. run, hit, fast, fall	FAST — NOT A VERB

THINGS	DIFFERENT THING

Here are some examples from **Science**.

	THINGS	DIFFERENT THING
21.	oak, pine, maple, ash	PINE — EVERGREEN
22.	peninsula, cape, gulf, island	GULF — NOT LAND
23.	skin, vein, hair, nail	VEIN — INSIDE BODY
24.	nylon, wax, polyester, teflon	WAX — NOT A PLASTIC
25.	cat, cow, dog, bear	BEAR — WILD ANIMAL
26.	mars, moon, earth, venus	MOON — NOT A PLANET
27.	frost, cloud, dust, dew	DUST — NOT WATER
28.	rat, guinea pig, mouse, ant eater	ANT EATER — NOT GNAWING ANIMAL
29.	heat, gas, sound, light	GAS — NOT ENERGY
30.	moon, sun, lamp, fire	MOON — REFLECTS BUT DOESN'T EMIT LIGHT
31.	electron, crystal, neutron, proton	CRYSTAL — NOT PART OF AN ATOM
32.	oxygen, nitrogen, carbon dioxide, hydrogen sulphide	HYDROGEN SULPHIDE — NOT A NATURAL GAS OF AIR
33.	fish, snake, worm, bird	WORM — NO BACKBONE
34.	stomach, mouth, lungs, intestine	LUNGS — NOT PART OF THE DIGESTIVE SYSTEMS

THINGS	DIFFERENT THING

Here are some things from **Social Studies**.

35.	president, mayor, governor, king	KING — NOT ELECTED
36.	judges, police soldiers, shopkeepers	SHOPKEEPERS — DON'T WORK FOR GOVERNMENT
37.	voter, dictator, representative, senator	DICTATOR — NOT PART OF A DEMOCRACY
38.	logging, mining, damming, replanting	REPLANTING — A PROCESS FOR CONSERVING
39.	oil, timber, coal, natural gas	TIMBER — RENEWABLE FUEL

6.   CLASSIFYING THINGS INTO CATEGORIES III

We all have a category in our brains that we label ANIMAL.

As we observe and read about new and different animals, we need to break our CATEGORY up into smaller, related categories.

In your brain you may have SMALLER or SUB-CATEGORIES of ANIMAL. For example, FARM ANIMALS, WILD ANIMALS, WATER ANIMALS, TREE CLIMBING ANIMALS, GRASS EATING ANIMALS and so on.

If we have to sort a large number of things of a common category into smaller categories, it is helpful to use a diagram. For example —

ANIMALS — elephants, cats, horses, monkeys, dogs, rabbits, tigers, cows, pigs,
(Category)   guinea pigs, zebras.

(Sub-categories)

WILD ANIMALS	HOUSE ANIMALS	FARM ANIMALS
elephants	cats	horses
monkeys	dogs	cows
lions	guinea pigs	
zebras		
rabbits		

THE FOLLOWING EXERCISES CONTAIN LISTS OF THINGS BELONGING TO A BIG, COMMON CATEGORY. BREAK THIS CATEGORY UP INTO **THREE** SMALLER CATEGORIES. WRITE **THE LABELS OF** THESE CATE-GORIES IN THE BOXES ☐ . SOME PEOPLE WILL USE DIFFER-ENT LABELS.

NOW WRITE UNDER THESE LABELS THE THINGS THAT BELONG TO THIS SMALL OR SUB-CATEGORY.

WHEN YOU HAVE FINISHED THE EXERCISES, GO BACK AND SEE IF YOU CAN BREAK EACH CATEGORY UP INTO **TWO** MORE CATEGORIES.

Here are some **common** things.

1. CLOTHING — hat, socks, sweater, cap, blouse, shoes, boots, shirt, tennis, shade

FOOTWEAR	HEADWEAR	BODY CLOTHES

Many answers possible. Use category headings as a guide.

2. FOOD — milk, carrots, cheese, apples, melon, potatoes, butter, cream, pears, berries, onions, bananas

FRUIT	VEGETABLES	DAIRY FOOD

3. SPORTS — Swimming, baseball, basketball, running, diving, high jump, soccer, hockey, sailing, shotput.

WATER SPORTS	ATHLETICS	BALL SPORTS

4. TOOLS — spade, plane, rake, saw, file, sander, chisel, hammer, shovel, mallet, sledge-hammer

GARDEN	HITTING	CUTTING

Here are some things from **Mathematics and Language Arts**.

5. MATHEMATICS — rectangle, meter, cylinder, cube, yard, mile, triangle, pyramid, square,
    CONCEPTS   kilometer, pentagon, sphere

UNIT	TWO-DIMENSIONAL	THREE DIMENSIONAL

6. WORDS — hat, drive, fast, door, heavy, fight, loud, apple, walk, climb, pretty, bed, pen.

NOUNS	VERBS	ADJECTIVES

Here are some things from **Science.**

7. BODY PARTS — intestine, kidney, bladder, nose, stomach, lungs, wind pipe, saliva, sweat, glands, mouth

DIGESTIVE	EXCRETORY	BREATHING

8. BIRDS — condor, ostrich, gull, eagle, swan, vulture, emu, kiwi, flamingo

OF PREY	WATER	FLIGHTLESS

9. SUBSTANCES — steel, water, air, plastic, oxygen, alcohol, carbon dioxide, wood, copper, kerosene, nitrogen, oil

SOLID	LIQUID	GAS

Here are some things from **Social Studies**.

10. OCCUPATIONS — journalist, lawyer, judge, cartoonist, secretary, sales person, actor, prison officer, sheriff, accountant, manager, news-reader

MEDIA	LAW	BUSINESS

11. OCCUPATIONS — rancher, nurse, actor, butcher, doctor, cook, writer, audience, ambulance driver, waiter, pharmacist, dentist

FOOD	HEALTH	FILM — MEDIA

12. ASSOCIATED WITH HUMANS — to eat, joy, car, to drink, a holiday, to sleep, jewelry, hate, jealousy

NEEDS	WANTS	EMOTIONS

7.   IDENTIFYING THE ESSENTIAL PROPERTIES OF A CONCEPT

In the last exercise we saw how big categories such as ANIMALS, CLOTHING, FOOD and SPORTS can be broken up into smaller categories.

Even though elephants, dogs and cows were placed into different Sub-categories, we still recognize all of them as ANIMALS.

In other words we must have a 'picture' in our brains of some ESSENTIAL PROPERTIES a thing must have before it is called an ANIMAL.

Before you call something an animal you might expect it to have a head, a body, legs, eyes and a mouth, to be living, and to be able to move.

These essential properties of your mental picture of an animal is called your CONCEPT of an animal. The word ANIMAL is the **label** you give to this mental picture or concept.

Different people may have other properties for their concept of an ANIMAL because they have SEEN more animals or read more about animals than you.

The aim of this exercise is to find out your concept (set of essential properties) of certain things.

WRITE DOWN THE **ESSENTIAL** PROPERTIES (CONCEPT) YOU HAVE IN YOUR BRAIN FOR THE FOLLOWING THINGS. REMEMBER, THESE PROPERTIES MUST BE COMMON TO **ALL** EXAMPLES OF EACH CONCEPT YOU HAVE OBSERVED SO FAR.

NOTE:

1.   WE MAY ALL HAVE A DIFFERENT CONCEPT OF THE SAME THING DEPENDING ON OUR EXPERIENCE AND OUR INTEREST IN THIS THING.

2.   IF IN FUTURE YOU FIND AN EXAMPLE OF SAY AN ANIMAL THAT DOESN'T FIT YOUR PRESENT MENTAL PICTURE (CONCEPT) OF AN ANIMAL, THEN YOU WILL HAVE TO CHANGE OR REFINE YOUR CONCEPT. USE CLASS OPINION AND THEIR MENTAL PICTURES TO REFINE YOUR ORIGINAL LISTS OF ESSENTIAL PROPERTIES. YOU WILL HAVE FUN ARGUING ABOUT THESE ESSENTIALS.

THING	ESSENTIAL PROPERTIES or CONCEPT
For example:	
a car	4 wheels, engine, steering wheel, brake, seat

THING	ESSENTIAL PROPERTIES or CONCEPT

Here are some **common** things.

1. a chair	FLAT SEAT, BACK SUPPORT
2. a coin	MADE OF METAL, ROUND, DATE, HEAD OF A LEADER, VALUE
3. a stamp	PAPER, STICKY BACK, PERFORATED EDGE, VALUE, COUNTRY

Here are some things from **Mathematics and Language Arts**.

4. a square	4 EQUAL SIDES, 4 RIGHT ANGLES, 2D, CLOSED FIGURE
5. a poem	CONTAINS WORDS, HAS ARTISTIC OR IMAGINATIVE THOUGHTS, HAS A SUBJECT
6. a word	HAS A SOUND, CAN BE WRITTEN, HAS MEANING BELONGS TO A LANGUAGE

Here are some things from **Science**.

7. a planet	SOLID, REFLECTS SUNLIGHT, MOVES AROUND SUN, TURNS ON AN AXIS, FOUND IN SPACE, CIRCULAR SHAPE

8. a bird

HAS 2 LEGS, 2 WINGS, WARM BLOODED, A BEAK, NO TEETH, A NEST, FEATHERS, BODY SYSTEMS

9. a flower

STEM, PETALS, STAMENS, COLORED, GROWS ON A BUSH/TREE, POLLEN ATTRACTS BEES

Here are some things from **Social Studies**.

10. a game

HAS RULES, A START AND A FINISH, PLAYED BY ONE OR MORE PEOPLE, INVOLVES ENJOYMENT

11. a law

MADE BY GOVERNMENT, POLICED, USED TO CONTROL PEOPLE, FINED IF BROKEN

12. a culture

WAYS OF A LARGE GROUP OF PEOPLE, HAS RELIGIONS, ARTS, FOOD AND CLOTHING

8. ORDERING CONCEPTS IN TERMS OF SIZE

We have seen how we all form mental pictures or concepts of things. Each of these concepts is given a label such as animal, tree, car, chair and so on.

For each concept there are some essential properties that are associated with it.

A large concept such as a house can be made up of smaller concepts such as **rooms** and **furniture** and so on.

It is interesting that in our brains we have stored related concepts in order of their size. We have told ourselves to remember that a house is larger than a room, and that a room is larger than a piece of furniture.

Sometimes the difference in size between related concepts is so small that it is difficult to place them in the correct order. This exercise tests how well you have ordered your related concepts.

IN THIS EXERCISE GROUPS OF RELATED CONCEPTS ARE GIVEN. YOU ARE ASKED TO RE—ORDER THEM SO THAT THE LARGEST CONCEPT IS GIVEN FIRST. THE SMALLEST CONCEPT SHOULD BE GIVEN LAST.

RELATED CONCEPTS	ORDER IN DECREASING SIZE
For example:	
sentence, paragraph, word	PARAGRAPH-SENTENCE-WORD

Now, here are some **common** things.

	RELATED CONCEPTS	ORDER IN DECREASING SIZE
1.	wheel, bicycle, spoke, transportation	TRANSPORTATION, BICYCLE, WHEEL, SPOKE
2.	bird, flock, wing, feather	FLOCK, BIRD, WING, FEATHER
3.	library, chapter, book, paragraph	LIBRARY, BOOK, CHAPTER, PARAGRAPH
4.	lane, highway, path, road	HIGHWAY, ROAD, LANE, PATH
5.	forest, twig, branch, tree	FOREST, TREE, BRANCH, TWIG

RELATED CONCEPTS	ORDER IN DECREASING SIZE
6. speech, act, scene, play	PLAY, ACT, SCENE, SPEECH

Here are some things from **Mathematics and Language**.

RELATED CONCEPTS	ORDER IN DECREASING SIZE
7. 0.01, 0.10, 1.00, 0.11	1.00, 0.11, 0.10, 0.01
8. 2/3, 19/36, 11/18, 5/9	2/3, 11/18, 5/9, 19/36
9. centimeter, kilometer, meter, millimeter	KILOMETER, METER, CENTIMETER, MILLIMETER
10. reflex angle, acute angle, right angle, obtuse angle	REFLEX ANGLE, OBTUSE ANGLE, RIGHT ANGLE, ACUTE ANGLE

Here are some things from **Science**.

RELATED CONCEPTS	ORDER IN DECREASING SIZE
11. planet, universe, moon, sun	UNIVERSE, SUN, PLANET, MOON
12. artery, blood system, body, heart	BODY, BLOOD SYSTEM, HEART, ARTERY
13. retina, eye, sensory system, rod	SENSORY SYSTEM, EYE, RETINA, ROD
14. crystal, atom, molecule, nucleus	CRYSTAL, MOLECULE, ATOM, NUCLEUS
15. body, cell, organ	BODY, ORGAN, CELL
16. capillaries, arteries, veins	ARTERIES, VEINS, CAPILLARIES

Here are things from **Social Studies**.

RELATED CONCEPTS	ORDER IN DECREASING SIZE
17. Asian, humanity, race, Chinese	HUMANITY, RACE, ASIAN, CHINESE
18. nation, daughter, family, community	NATION, COMMUNITY, FAMILY, DAUGHTER
19. tribe, family, race, son	RACE, TRIBE, FAMILY, SON

RELATED CONCEPTS	ORDER IN DECREASING SIZE
20. senator, government, party, nation	NATION, GOVERNMENT, PARTY, SENATOR
21. Catholic, priest, culture, religion	CULTURE, RELIGION, CATHOLIC, PRIEST
22. town, suburb, country, state	COUNTRY, STATE, TOWN, SUBURB

9. ORDERING CONCEPTS IN TERMS OF TIME

Concepts that are related to each other can often be placed in a SEQUENCE, or in some particular ORDER. We even store this sequence in our brains along with the related concepts.

The order might be:

1) from the smallest thing to the largest thing.

2) from the action occurring first to the action occurring last.

or 3) in terms of cost, weight, acidity, age, and many other criteria.

THE FOLLOWING RELATED CONCEPTS ARE MIXED UP. RE—ORDER THEM BY PLACING THE THINGS THAT OCCUR FIRST AT THE BEGINNING AND THE THINGS THAT OCCUR LAST AT THE END.

RELATED CONCEPTS	ORDER FIRST TO LAST OCCURRING
For example:	
save — spend — earn	EARN, SAVE, SPEND

Here are some **common** things to place in order.

1. hang up — talk — dial	DIAL, TALK, HANG UP
2. bait — reel in — cast	BAIT, CAST, REEL IN
3. seed — plough — harvest	PLOUGH, SEED, HARVEST
4. fire — load — aim	LOAD, AIM, FIRE
5. seal — write — post — deliver	WRITE, SEAL, POST, DELIVER
6. mount — ride — harness	HARNESS, MOUNT, RIDE
7. compete — train — win	TRAIN, COMPETE, WIN

RELATED CONCEPTS	ORDER FIRST TO LAST OCCURRING
8. cut — sew — measure	MEASURE, CUT, SEW

Here are some things from **Science**.

RELATED CONCEPTS	ORDER FIRST TO LAST OCCURRING
9. dusk — mid-day — dawn — midnight	DAWN, MID-DAY, DUSK, MIDNIGHT
10. thunder — flood — rain — lightning	LIGHTNING, THUNDER, RAIN, FLOOD
11. caterpillar — egg — butterfly	BUTTERFLY, EGG, CATERPILLAR
12. summer — winter — spring	WINTER, SPRING, SUMMER
13. car — hovercraft — plane — bicycle	BICYCLE, CAR, PLANE, HOVERCRAFT
14. clock — sun — sundial — sand timer	SUN, SUNDIAL, SAND TIMER, CLOCK

Here are some things from **Social Studies**.

RELATED CONCEPTS	ORDER FIRST TO LAST OCCURRING
15. election — nomination — campaign	NOMINATION, CAMPAIGN, ELECTION
16. invent — sell — manufacture — research	RESEARCH, INVENT, MANUFACTURE, SELL
17. compose — rehearse — perform	COMPOSE, REHEARSE, PERFORM
18. spin — weave — shear — tailor	SHEAR, SPIN, WEAVE, TAILOR
19. mill — harvest — bake — eat	HARVEST, MILL, BAKE, EAT
20. landscape — design — paint — build	DESIGN, BUILD, PAINT, LANDSCAPE
21. sell — advertise — manufacture — purchase	MANUFACTURE, ADVERTISE, SELL, PURCHASE

ANALYZING SKILLS

Exercises 10-15 aim to help you identify and distinguish between parts and properties of things.

The skills include —

Identifying properties and parts.
Identifying relationships and patterns.

10. IDENTIFYING RELATIONSHIPS

An analogy has TWO PAIRS OF CONCEPTS that make the same relationship. For example.

FINGER is to HAND as TOE is to FOOT

The finger is part of the hand.
The toe is part of the foot.

To see if you can think about how concepts are related, we will leave one concept out of each analogy.

For example:

SCISSORS are to PAPER as SAW is to _____

TO COMPLETE AN ANALOGY —

- Think how the first concept e.g. scissors is related to the second concept e.g. paper.

- Relationship: scissors are used to **cut** paper.

- Now the third concept e.g. saw, must also be able to **cut** the missing concept.

- Missing concept could be **wood** or **metal**.

WRITE IN THE MISSING CONCEPT TO COMPLETE THE FOLLOWING ANALOGIES.

Here are some common things

1. GLOVES are to HANDS as	SOCKS are to	FEET
2. SHIPS are to SEA as	PLANES are to	AIR
3. BOOK is to PAPER as	TIRE is to	RUBBER
4. EAGLE is to BIRD as	RED is to	COLOR
5. BIRD is to WING as	FISH is to	FIN
6. CUP is to SAUCER as	KNIFE is to	FORK

Here are some things from **Mathematics and Language Arts**.

7.	ANGLE is to TRIANGLE as	WORD is to	SENTENCE
8.	12 is to 144 as	6 is to	36 or 72
9.	CIRCLE is to SPHERE as	SQUARE is to	CUBE
10.	WENT is to VERB as	DOG is to	NOUN
11.	SMILES is to SMILED as	RUNS is to	RAN
12.	3 is to 4 as	75 is to	100
13.	MILLIMETER is to METER as	METER is to	KILOMETER
14.	TRIANGLE is to THREE as	HEXAGON is to	SIX
15.	AUTHOR is to WRITE as	ACTOR is to	ACT
16.	SING is to SANG as	RIDE is to	RODE

Here are some examples from **Science** .

17.	OAK is to DECIDUOUS as	PINE is to	EVERGREEN
18.	OXYGEN is to SODIUM CHLORIDE as	ELEMENT is to	COMPOUND
19.	MOON is to PLANET as	ELECTRON is to	NUCLEUS
20.	HEAT is to ENERGY as	PUSH is to	FORCE
21.	STOMACH is to DIGESTION as	LUNGS are to	BREATHING
22.	SUN is to STAR as	EARTH is to	PLANET
23.	ARTERY is to BLOOD as	NERVE is to	ELECTRICITY
24.	RETINA is to EYE as	VENTRICLE is to	HEART

Here are some examples from **Social Studies**.

25.	PRESIDENT is to NATION as	MAYOR is to	CITY
26.	EAT is to NEED as	WEALTH is to	WANT
27.	CHINESE is to ASIAN as	CATHOLIC is to	RELIGION
28.	RULE is to GAME as	LAW is to	SOCIETY
29.	SHERIFF is to LAW as	MANAGER is to	BUSINESS
30.	JUDGE is to COURT as	ARTIST is to	STUDIO

11. IDENTIFYING PATTERNS IN SEQUENCES

The members of a figure sequence can differ slightly from each other in a particular way.

Look at the examples below:

1. — a **PROGRESSIVE** change.

Here each member shows a **gradual** change from the member on either side of it. The size, shape, direction, color and other properties can change gradually.

2. — an **ALTERNATING** change.

Here the uneven numbered members of the sequence are the same. The even numbered members are all the same but different from the uneven numbered members.

3.  — a **ROTATING** change.

Here each member is turned either clockwise or anticlockwise from the previous member.

Look at the following sequences carefully.

Now —

---

1. WRITE IN **WHAT TYPE** OF CHANGE IS OCCURRING IN EACH SEQUENCE.

2. DRAW IN THE MISSING MEMBER OF EACH SEQUENCE.

SEQUENCE	TYPE OF CHANGE
1.	ROTATING
2.	PROGRESSIVE

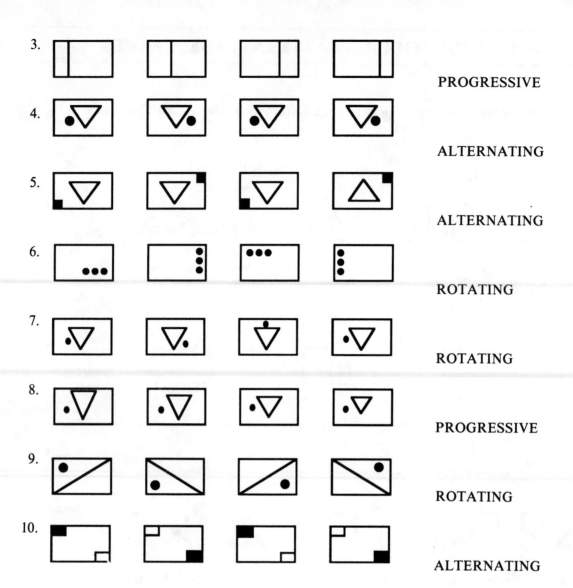

3.   PROGRESSIVE

4.   ALTERNATING

5.   ALTERNATING

6.   ROTATING

7.   ROTATING

8.   PROGRESSIVE

9.   ROTATING

10.   ALTERNATING

In the previous exercise we saw how the members of a sequence change in a regular pattern. When trying to find this pattern do the following.

1) Look carefully at the parts making up each member of the sequence, e.g. AAB, AFGA, 62.

2) Look carefully at two members of the sequence that are next to each other and see how the parts of each member have changed.

e.g. AB and AC	second part increased by one letter of alphabet.
10 and 12	first part increased by 2
10 and 8	second member decreased by 2
10 and 30	second member multiplied by 3

3) Check another two members of the sequence to make sure that the pattern of change that you have identified is still the same.

IN THE FOLLOWING SEQUENCES ONE MEMBER IS MISSING.

WRITE IN THE MISSING MEMBER. MAKE SURE YOU FIND THE PATTERN IN THE SEQUENCE FIRST.

1.	(A A Z)	A A Y		A A X		A A W
2.	A B	B B		(C B)		D B
3.	O O	(P P)		Q Q		R R
4.	Z Z	Y Y		(X X)		W W
5.	A C	C C		(E C)		G C
6.	C A H	C B H		(C C H)		C D H
7.	B Y B	C Y C		(D Y D)		E Y E
8.	A F G A	B F G B		C F G C		(D F G D)
9.	4	9	16	(24)	36	49
10.	3	4	6	9	13	(17)
11.	2	7 .	10	15	18	(23)

35

| 12. | 24 | 20 | 18 | 14 | (10) | 8 |
| 13. | 2 | 4 | 8 | 16 | 32 | (60) |

In the last six items the members of the sequence are hidden. You have to circle each member or collection of figures when you find it being repeated. Then draw in the missing figure for the member which contains the missing part.

14.

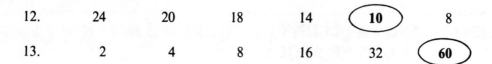

15.

16.

17.

18.

19.

36

Write down all the possible uses for a BRICK.

Most people would only write down *to build* ... a house, a church, a wall and so on. Only **one category of ideas** — namely to build a vertical structure.

Creative or flexible thinkers think about things in alternative ways. They can 'picture' different properties of things in their minds.

For example, to them a BRICK is more than something solid to build things with. Let us list some other properties of a brick.

HARD

HEAVY

ROUGH

GEOMETRIC SHAPE

Now what can HARD things be used for?

As a **weapon**, as a hammer, ...

What can HEAVY things be used for?

As a paper weight, doorstop, shotput, anchor, weight lifting, ...

What can ROUGH things be used for?

To sharpen knives, pencils, ...

What can GEOMETRIC solids be used for?

As a border, a paving stone, a tire wedge, a bookshelf support, ...

Flexible thinkers are really "shifting mental gears" from one category of use to another. They are not locked into only one way of looking at something.

LIST SOME PROPERTIES OF THE FOLLOWING THINGS.
THEN TRY TO SUGGEST AS MANY DIFFERENT USES FOR THEM
AS YOU CAN.

1. A newspaper.

PROPERTIES	POSSIBLE USES
porous	WIPING, BLOTTING
burns easily	AS A FUEL
easily rolled	A SWAT OR WEDGE
soft	TO WRAP BREAKABLES
large surface area	TO COVER FLOORS, BOOKS
easily torn	GARDEN MULCH
printed	TO READ

2. A piece of string.

PROPERTIES	POSSIBLE USES
thin / long	TO TIE THINGS, TO SEW THINGS, TO WEAVE, THREAD BEADS
strong	SHOE LACE, A BELT, A WASHING LINE

3. A thumb tack.

PROPERTIES	POSSIBLE USES
small, round	TO COVER A HOLE
metallic with spike	TIP OF A SHOE, A SPINNING TOP, TO PIN PAPER

All of the things about us that have been made by human beings, were **invented** by someone many years ago.

Somewhere in the past a person first invented a screw, a pencil, a comb, some matches, a paint brush, a wheel, a telephone, a radio, and so on.

Today we take most of these things for granted.
You can share in the creativity of these inventors by doing a PMS on a past invention.

In doing so you might start to think like these early inventors and to ask yourself some questions that they asked themselves.

What is PMS?

It is a careful look at the **parts** (P), the **materials** it is made from (M), and the **structure** or **shape** (S) of the invention.

Ask yourself these questions about an invention.

1.   What are the different parts used for?

2.   Why is it made of this particular material?

3.   Why is it the shape that it is?

DO A PMS ANALYSIS OF THE COMMON INVENTIONS BELOW.
THINK ABOUT AND WRITE DOWN ANSWERS TO THE THREE
QUESTIONS ABOVE.

---

1. A PENCIL

PARTS	USE OF EACH PART
WOODEN STICK	TO HOLD, TO KEEP HANDS CLEAN, TO PROTECT LEAD
WRITING LEAD	TO MARK PAPER

MATERIAL(S) OF PARTS	WHY IS THIS MATERIAL CHOSEN?
WOOD (STICK)	EASY TO SHARPEN, CHEAP, LIGHT, EASY TO SHAPE, SOFT TO GRIP
GRAPHITE (LEAD)	EASY TO MOLD, STRONG, BLACK, MARKS CLEARLY

SHAPE	WHY WAS THIS SHAPE CHOSEN?
SIX SIDED STICK	EASY TO GRIP AND PACK, DOESN'T ROLL EASILY
LONG STICK	LASTS LONGER
ROUND LEAD	STRONG, EASY TO MOLD
THIN LEAD	TO PRODUCE A THIN LINE

2. SAFETY MATCHES

PARTS	USE OF EACH PART
STICK	TO BURN AND HOLD
HEAD	TO SUPPLY FLAME
BOX	TO STORE AND PROTECT MATCHES TO SUPPLY FRICTION TO HEAD

MATERIAL(S) OF PARTS	WHY IS THIS MATERIAL CHOSEN?
WOOD — STICK	BURNS EASILY, CHEAP, LIGHT
CHEMICALS — HEAD	IGNITES WHEN HOT
CARDBOARD — BOX	EASY TO FOLD/PRINT/DESTROY

SHAPE	WHY WAS THIS SHAPE CHOSEN?
STRAIGHT STICK	EASY TO CUT, HOLD, STORE
ROUND HEAD	EASY TO RUB ON BOX WITHOUT BREAKING
RECTANGULAR BOX	EASY TO FOLD, STORE

3. A SODA BOTTLE

PARTS	USE OF EACH PART
BOTTLE	TO STORE LIQUID
CAP	TO KEEP AIR OUT — LIQUID IN
LABEL	TO NAME CONTENTS

MATERIAL(S) OF PARTS	WHY IS THIS MATERIAL CHOSEN?
GLASS BOTTLE	EASY TO CLEAN, SEE THROUGH, MAKE
METAL CAP	DOESN'T CORRODE, AIR TIGHT
PAPER LABEL	PRINT ON EASILY

SHAPE	WHY WAS THIS SHAPE CHOSEN?
CYLINDRICAL BOTTLE	STRONG, EASY TO MAKE/STORE
SCREW THREAD TOP	MAKES A GOOD SEAL

15.   THINKING ABOUT CREATIVE STRUCTURES

Think about some of the strong structures that you have seen. These might include buildings, bridges and tall supporting posts. You may have noticed that curved surfaces such as cylinders and spheres are used because they are stronger than flat surfaces.

This exercise requires you to think creatively about possible structures.

IN EACH OF THE FOLLOWING DESIGN PROBLEMS, ALL YOU CAN USE IS ONE SHEET OF A4 (30cm. x 20cm.) PAPER AND NO MORE THAN 25cm. (12″) OF STICKY TAPE.
BUILD A STRUCTURE FOR EACH SET OF REQUIREMENTS GIVEN.
DO THIS WITH A SMALL TEAM OF STUDENTS.

---

1. **PROBLEM**

   Build a structure that will support a text book, at least 5 centimeters (2″) above a desk top. The book should be no less 2.5 centimeters (1″) thick.

2. **PROBLEM**

   Build **the tallest structure** you can that will stand by itself without anything or anybody holding it.

3. **PROBLEM**

   Build a three dimensional shape with the **largest surface area** possible. Check your area with the aid of a mathematics formula.

GENERATING SKILLS

Exercises 16-25 aim to help you make connections between new and old information. Your old information is used to add meaning and new information to things you are exposed to.

Inferring/ Predicting	drawing tentative conclusions about things you sense are or could be true.
Representing	using visuals to show how information is related.
Elaborating	using previous knowledge to add meaning to new information.

16.   REPRESENTING RELATED CONCEPTS

Many related concepts of differing size are often introduced to you in a lesson or in a chapter of a book.

Sometimes it helps you to picture how they are related if you draw a diagram. This can be called a *concept map*.

At the end of a lesson or a homework reading do the following:

1.   List all the key terms/words/concepts.

2.   Re-order them so that the biggest concept is first and the smallest last.

3.   Draw an arrow to join related concepts. Use a few words on the arrow to show how the concepts are related.

EXAMPLE

1.   Here are some related concepts from a lesson on TREES:

Leaves, trunk, roots, carbon dioxide, trees, starch, branches, water.

2.   Here are the concepts placed in approximate order of their SIZE.

Trees, trunk, branches, roots, leaves, carbon dioxide, starch.

3.   Here is a diagram or map of the concepts showing how they are related.

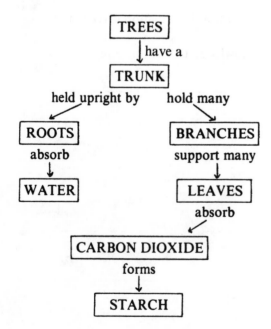

NOTE:

- Concepts are boxed.
- Biggest concept at the top.
- Concepts gradually get smaller down the chain.

- You might have to draw more than one chain.

Different people will draw different concept maps. You will use different connecting words. You will place concepts in slightly different order.

USE THE EXAMPLE AND DRAW CONCEPT MAPS FOR THE FOL-
LOWING LISTS OF JUMBLED CONCEPTS.

Here are some **common** things.

1. sentences, words, pages, books, library, chapters, shelves, school.

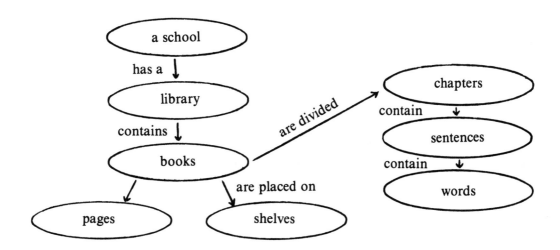

2. shells, ocean, fish, crabs, sand, rocks, beach, waves, reef.

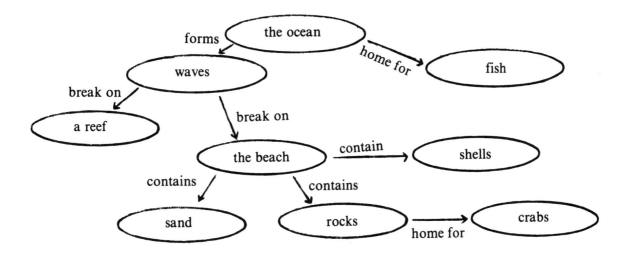

Here are some things from **Mathematics**.

3. squares, sides, circles, closed figures, polygons, diameters, rectangles, segments, diagonals, quadrilaterals.

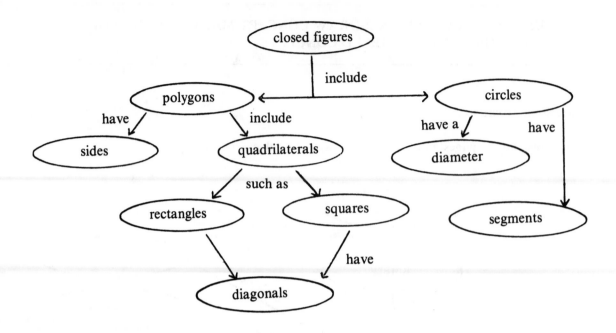

Here are some things from **Science**.

4. Heart, human body, oxygen, veins, breathing system, arteries, blood, blood system, nose, carbon dioxide, lungs.

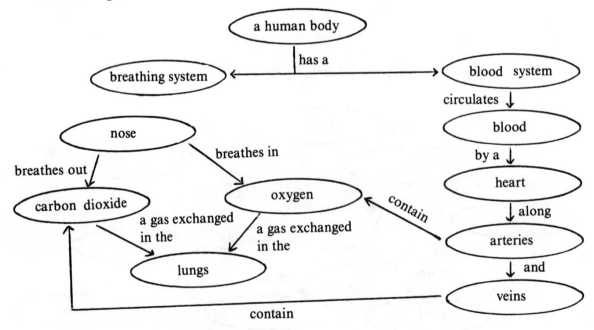

Here are some things from **Social Studies**.

5. voters, government, elections, states, senators, departments, political parties, representatives, health, treasury.

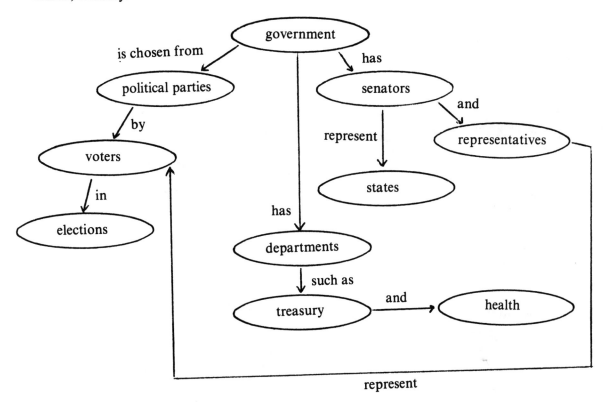

17.   REPRESENTING THINGS WITH SHARED PROPERTIES

Let us look at the properties of some shapes.

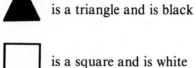 is a triangle and is black

is a square and is white

We can represent a set or group of black things by putting them inside a circle.   e.g.

BLACK
SHAPES

We can represent a set or group of squares of any color by putting them inside another circle   e.g.

SQUARES

Now overlap our circles or sets of things

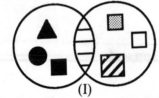

What does the shaded area (1) represent?
It is part of squares (S) and it is part of black shapes (B)
Therefore it must represent — BLACK SQUARES

(I)
BLACK SHAPES   SQUARES
(B)   (S)

Where would you put the following shapes — in S, B or I?

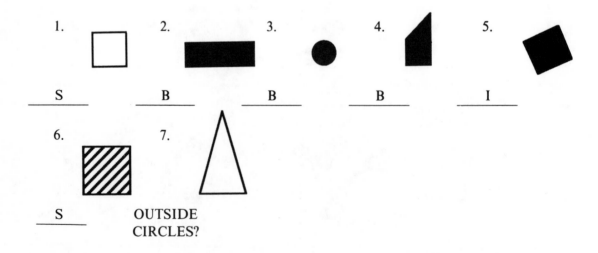

1.   2.   3.   4.   5.

S   B   B   B   I

6.   7.

S   OUTSIDE
                     CIRCLES?

48

Consider three sets

P   C

A

Here is how he can show the following statements

NO CATS ARE PURPLE

keep circles **SEPARATE**

ALL CATS ARE ANIMALS

Draw the CATS in a small circle and place it anywhere **INSIDE** the larger circle for ANIMALS.

SOME ANIMALS ARE PURPLE

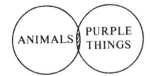

OVERLAP the circle for animals with the circle for purple things. The shaded area represents purple animals.

DRAW DIAGRAMS TO REPRESENT THE FOLLOWING STATEMENTS.

---

1. Some geometric shapes (G) are small things (S)

2. All adjectives (A) are words (W)

3. No verbs (V) are nouns (N)

4. All sentences (S) contain nouns (N).
   All languages (L) contain sentences

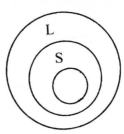

5. The category of fish (F) does not include birds (B)

6. All politicians (P) are human beings (H)
   Some politicans are women (W)

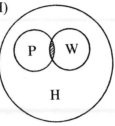

7. Some animals (A) have legs (L)
   Some animals (A) have wings (W)

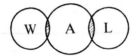

The diagram below shows how THREE categories or properties can be related.

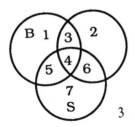

B represents BLACK things
(areas 1, 3, 4, 5)
T represents TRIANGLES
(areas 2, 3, 4, 6)
S represents SMALL things
(areas 7, 5, 4, 6)

Black triangles are represented by areas 3 & 4.
Black small things are represented by areas 5 & 4.
Small triangles are represented by areas 4 & 6.
Small, black, triangles are represented by area 4.

Which area represents

1. Small white triangles?   6

2. Large black triangles?   3

3. Small black circles?   5

4. Large shaded triangles?   2

1. In the diagram opposite

    A represents animals

    L represents animals with legs

    W represents animals with wings.

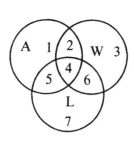

Which numbered area or areas represent

1.	Ducks	4
2.	Horses	5
3.	Fish	1
4.	Snakes	1
5.	Ants	5 or 4
6.	Moths	4

2. In the diagram opposite

    A represents geometric figures with all angles equal

    S represents geometric figures with all sides equal

    F represents geometric figures with four sides

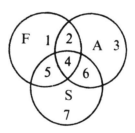

Which numbered area or areas represent

1.	Squares	4
2.	Parallelograms	1
3.	Rhombuses	5
4.	Pentagons	6
5.	Isosceles triangles	NIL

3. **In the diagram opposite**

A represents American people

W represents white skinned people

F represents females

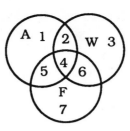

Which numbered area or areas represent

1. Abraham Lincoln   2

2. The Queen of England   6

3. Martin Luther King   1

4. The head of Russia   3

5. Film star Elizabeth Taylor   4

18.   ELABORATING MEANING TO NEW WORDS

We have seen how we use our brain to make links between different concepts that are often related or used together.

Sometimes we read a sentence with a word for a concept that we don't know. We haven't seen it before. We know the surrounding words but not this new one.

Some people skip over the words. They don't want to learn new words of their language. Some people will look up the word immediately in a dictionary to find out what it means. They now have a new word in their vocabulary.

People without a dictionary at hand can guess the meaning of a new word from the sentence or paragraph it is in. If you stop to think about or draw mental picture of the words on either side of the new word you can usually correctly guess the meaning of your new word.

EXAMPLE

He drove the zonk down the road. It had big tires to hold the weight of forty passengers.

Did you guess that a zonk is probably a bus?

TRY TO GUESS THE MEANING OF THE WORDS IN BOLD IN THE FOLLOWING SENTENCES. READ EACH SENTENCE THROUGH AND TRY TO PICTURE THE THINGS AND THE SETTING.

---

1)   The **buckeye** grows to about forty feet high and has nuts that look like the eye of a male deer.

A TREE

2)   Jim was **obese**. He obviously did little exercise and loved to eat many cakes and doughnuts.

FAT

3)   Jean didn't like to be out in the sun. She bought a **fez** to wear whenever she walked outside.

A HAT

4.   The girl climbed the **coquito** as it swayed gently in the breeze.

A TREE

5.   The **malamute** lifted its ears and listened for a command. The snow collected on the fur around its back.

A DOG

6. The girl picked the **edelweiss** that was blooming on the hillside.

A FLOWER

7. The **stickleback** swam between the reeds. The dog avoided the thorny spines along its small, slippery back.

A FISH

8. The **gingham** was dyed a brown color and then cut to form a large shirt.

CLOTH OR FABRIC

9. The men pulled the **siene** around the school of fish. Many fish were caught this way.

A NET

10. The **widgeon** flew from its nest in the reeds and landed on the still lake.

A DUCK

11. The old lady made a loud sound with her **sabots** as she walked on the street. The grain on the sabots had worn away on the outsides. She would need a new pair soon.

WOODEN SHOES

12. The girl used a **piastre** to enter the gates of the bull fighting stadium.

A COIN

13. The **terrapin** swam to the shore. On land its shell protected it from the dogs.

A TORTOISE

14. Mr. Jones gave his sermon in the **kirk**. The **kirk** was built in 1803.

A CHURCH

15. The soldiers rode their horses through the gates of the **presidio** for protection from the attacking Indians.

A WALLED FORT

16. The boy hooked the **plaice** and pulled it out from the sea onto the jetty.

A FISH

17. The **raptor** swept down from the cliff to pick up the mouse in its claws and sharp beak.

A BIRD OF PREY

18. The wind was strong and the **sloop** bent over as it passed around the marker buoy.

A BOAT

19. The servant crushed the dried **beladonna** leaves. He hid the powder in his drawer to use on the King the following day.

A POISONOUS FLOWER

Now use a dictionary to find some difficult words. Make up a sentence with each word that you choose. See if your friends can think up the meaning of the words you have chosen and underlined in your sentences.

Sometimes we can't solve problems because we can't follow instructions carefully. These instructions can be given by the teacher or written in a book.

CAREFULLY READ THE FOLLOWING INSTRUCTIONS.
UNDERLINE THE IMPORTANT THINGS IN EACH INSTRUCTION
THAT YOU HAVE TO PAY ATTENTION TO.
THEN CARRY OUT THE INSTRUCTION.

---

1. Cross out the last two numbers

    2 6 5 4 9 8 7̸ 2̸.

2. Circled the middle number

    4 6 5 ④ 9 2 1

3. Underline the third and fifth letter

    A G K̲ L X̲ N P

4. Cross out the even numbers

    3 4̸ 1 3 6̸ 8̸ 9 7 2̸ 1

5. Circle the vowels

    G H J Ⓐ K X Ⓞ Ⓞ P Ⓤ S Ⓐ

6. Draw a square. Inside the top left corner draw a question mark.

    ┌─────────┐
    │ **?**   │
    │   │
    └─────────┘

7. Write down what you would say to someone if you wanted them
    to draw this figure without seeing it.

    DRAW A SQUARE WITH SIDES 2 CMS, THE BASE
    SHOULD BE PARALLEL TO THE BOTTOM OF THE
    PAGE. ON THE UPPER SIDE DRAW AN EQUILATERAL
    TRIANGLE. ON THE RIGHT SIDE OF THE SQUARE
    DRAW A SEMI-CIRCLE WITH THE SIDE AS ITS
    DIAMETER.

8.

4th Avenue | 5th Avenue | 6th Avenue

1st Street

2nd Street

3rd Street

X
START

You are at X. Draw your path if you walk.
1.   One block north.
2.   Two blocks east.
3.   One block south.
4.   One block west.
On the corner of which two streets will you be?
THIRD STREET AND FIFTH AVENUE

How far and in which direction do you need to walk to return to the START?
ONE BLOCK DUE WEST

9.   Draw a square. In the upper left corner draw a circle.
     In the corner below the circle draw a triangle.

10. Draw a circle. In the circle draw a square.
     One the left of the square and inside the circle draw a triangle.

11. In the diagram opposite the figures are lying top of each other.
     The bottom figure is the CIRCLE.

12. Draw three unequal size squares alongside each other in a
     straight line.
     The biggest square is in the middle, the smallest on the left of it.

13. Draw three squares so that they look as though they are lying on
     top of each other. The biggest is on top and the smallest is on
     the bottom.

14. Draw a square. Draw a circle outside the square but touching the top edge of the square. Draw a triangle inside the square with its base on the bottom edge of the square.

15. Draw a circle. Draw a square outside the circle with all of its sides touching the circle. Now draw another circle outside the square so that it touches the four corners of the square.

16. Draw three squares with each side about 2 cms.
The first square is at the top of a page and in the center. The second square is joined to this top square. The top righthand corner of the second square is in the middle of the bottom side of the top square. The top left corner of the third square touches the bottom right corner of the second square.

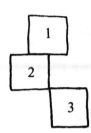

20.   REPRESENTING 'NO, ALL and SOME' STATEMENTS

We can use circles to represent a concept or a category.

For example represents all dogs or the category of dogs.

We can also use circles to represent a statement that states how pairs of concepts are related.

For example

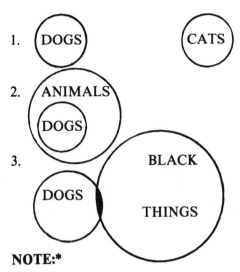

1.   represents the statement that
NO DOGS ARE CATS

2.   represents the statement
ALL DOGS ARE ANIMALS

3.   represents the statement
SOME DOGS ARE BLACK THINGS

NOTE:*

From diagram 1 :   * If **NO DOGS ARE CATS it is also true that NO CATS ARE DOGS.**

From diagram 2 :   * If **ALL** DOGS ARE ANIMALS **it is also true that** ALL ANIMALS ARE **NOT** dogs.

From diagram 3 :   * If **SOME** DOGS ARE BLACK THINGS **it is also true that** SOME BLACK THINGS ARE DOGS.

Finally, we can also use circles to show how concepts in TWO statements are related. A combination of our circles allow us to make some conclusions about how the concepts are related.

For example

Statement 1   All terriers (T) are dogs (D)

Statement 2   All dogs (D) are animals (A).

Because from 1   D includes all T

The diagram for Statement 2 can be shown as

Now our conclusions are

1) All terriers (T) are animals (A).
2) Some animals are dogs.
3) Some animals are terriers.
4) Some dogs are terriers.

2.   Statement 1.   Some black things (B) are dogs (D).

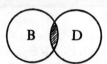

Statement 2.   All dogs (D) are animals (A).

Because from 1 some of D contains B.
The diagram for Statement 2 can be shown as

Now our conclusions are

1) Some black things (B) are animals (A).
2) Some animals (A) are black things (B).

USE CIRCLES TO REPRESENT THE FOLLOWING STATEMENTS. WHERE TWO CIRCLES ARE COMBINED WRITE DOWN THE CONCLUSIONS YOU MAKE FROM THE TWO STATEMENTS.

EXERCISES

1. No circles (C) are squares (S)

2. All carrots (C) are vegetables (V)

3. Some men (M) are blue eyed humans (BH)

4. Some politicians (P) are women (W)
    All women are human beings (H)

ALL POLITICIANS ARE HUMAN BEINGS

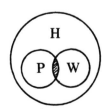

61

5. All bees (B) are insects (I)
    All insects are animals (A)

ALL BEES ARE ANIMALS
SOME ANIMALS ARE INSECTS
SOME ANIMALS ARE BEES

6. All terriers (T) are dogs (D)
    No dogs are cats (C)

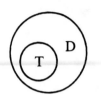

NO TERRIERS ARE CATS

7. All squares (S) are quadrilaterals (Q)
    No triangles (T) are quadrilaterals

NO TRIANGLES ARE SQUARES

21.   MAKING INFERENCES FROM OBSERVATIONS

An inference is a **CONCLUSION** you make after seeing or hearing something. Your inference may be **CORRECT OR INCORRECT**.

The **MORE TIMES** you see or hear the same thing the more likely your inference will be correct. If you make an inference after seeing or hearing something only once, then you are probably **ASSUMING** that certain things are true. You are making some assumptions.

For example, if you see a fruit tree with most of the fruit on the ground under it, various things could have happened.

1)   A strong wind could have blown the fruit off.
2)   A vandal could have pulled the fruit off.
3)   Some animals or birds may have pulled the fruit off.

You may **infer** or conclude that a **vandal pulled** the fruit off.
If this is your **inference** then the other two possibilities become assumptions. In other words **you are assuming** that a **strong wind** or **birds or animals** were **not the causes.**

An inference is your preferred conclusion. Assumptions are other possible conclusions that you think are less likely.

WRITE DOWN SOME INFERENCES THAT PEOPLE MIGHT MAKE WHEN THEY SEE THE FOLLOWING SITUATIONS.
IF YOU CAN ONLY MAKE ONE INFERENCE, LISTEN TO THOSE OF OTHER STUDENTS. THESE ARE YOUR ASSUMPTIONS.

OBSERVATIONS	POSSIBLE INFERENCES
1. Your flashlight won't work when you switch it on.	SWITCH BROKEN GLOBE BROKEN BATTERIES FLAT
2. The hardware store is having a closing down sale.	STORE TO BE DEMOLISHED OWNER DIED OWNER BANKRUPT

63

Here are some observations from **Mathematics, Science and Social Studies**.

OBSERVATIONS	POSSIBLE INFERENCES
3. More Math students are using calculators in Math classes today than they did ten years ago.	CALCULATORS CHEAP NOW PUBLIC ACCEPT CALCULATORS CALCULATORS IMPORTANT TOOL IN ADULT WORK
4. Panda bears are almost extinct now.	PANDAS DON'T REPRODUCE EASILY PANDAS ARE DYING FROM A VIRUS FOOD SUPPLY IS RUNNING OUT PANDAS HAVE ALMOST BEEN KILLED OFF BY HUMANS AND PREDATORS
5. The number of nuclear power stations in the world increases each year.	WORLD IS RUNNING OUT OF OIL AND COAL IT IS CHEAPER TO PRODUCE ELECTRICITY FROM URANIUM IT IS CLEANER TO PRODUCE ELECTRICITY FROM URANIUM
6. In some countries it is against the law to use Freon Gas in pressure can sprays.	FREON CAN CAUSE SICKNESS WE ARE RUNNING OUT OF FREON GAS FREON IS DAMAGING THE ATMOSPHERE

SITUATIONS	POSSIBLE INFERENCES
7. University students are protesting in the streets against the Government destroying forests for making woodchips.	UNIVERSITY STUDENTS LIKE PROTESTING FORESTS ARE IMPORTANT TO HUMAN BEINGS FORESTS ARE PROFITABLE FOR GOVERNMENTS
8. On the supermarket shelf Brand X soap has 3 soaps per pack for $1.20. Brand Y has 3 soaps per pack for $1.00	BRAND Y IS OF BETTER VALUE BRAND Y IS OF POORER QUALITY BRAND Y IS NOT SELLING TOO WELL.
9. Two different animal tracks go into a burrow. Only one set of these tracks come out of a burrow next to the first burrow.	ONE ANIMAL KILLED THE OTHER ONE ANIMAL IS HIDING INSIDE THE TWO BURROWS ARE NOT CONNECTED
10. The sidewalk outside the front of Joe's Pizza shop is always covered with litter. The sidewalk outside the front of Jim's Pizza shop nearby is always neat and free of litter.	JIM IS TIDIER THAN JOE MORE PEOPLE EAT AT JOE'S JIM'S CUSTOMERS ARE TIDIER THAN JOE'S CUSTOMERS ARE

22. MAKING INFERENCES FROM ADVERTISEMENTS

Advertisements in newspapers, magazines, and T.V. try to get us to buy or do something that we normally wouldn't. The advertisements use statements that are true. However, they are easily misinterpreted by the reader.

We all draw conclusions or inferences after reading advertisements.

The innocent, unthinking reader draws a "nice" inference. This is the inference the advertising agent hopes for.

The cautious, thinking reader draws a "mean" inference. This inference is usually correct or is the real situation. The "mean" inference can still be true even though it is extreme.

EXAMPLE

"Greg Norman drinks COLA RITE."

WHAT DID YOU INFER ABOUT —	NICE INFERENCE	MEAN INFERENCE (POSSIBLY THE TRUTH)
how **often** Greg drinks COLA RITE?	every day or regularly	once a year
why Greg **chose** COLA RITE?	because he likes the taste	because he is paid to drink it.
why COLA RITE is being advertised?	it is a new drink	the sales of COLA RITE are down.

WRITE A NICE INFERENCE AND A MEAN INFERENCE (USUALLY TRUE) FOR THE FOLLOWING ADVERTISEMENTS.

1. "The bicycles at this shop will be sold at only a fraction of the cost."

WHAT DID YOU INFER ABOUT —	NICE INFERENCE	MEAN INFERENCE (POSSIBLY THE TRUTH)
the **number** of cycles to be sold?	ALL CYCLES	A FEW SLOW-SELLING BICYCLES
the **size** of the fraction?	AT LEAST 50% OFF	1% or 2% OFF

66

2. "Smart kids are changing over to Skido bikes."

WHAT DID YOU INFER ABOUT —	NICE INFERENCE	MEAN INFERENCE (POSSIBLY THE TRUTH)
the meaning of **smart**?	CLEVER	SPOILED, RICH
the **number** of kids changing?	LARGE % OF BUYERS	A SMALL NUMBER
how the advertiser **knows** this is true?	THROUGH MARKET SURVEY	DOESN'T HAVE ANY EVIDENCE

3. "Own your own home only minutes from the city."

WHAT DID YOU INFER ABOUT —	NICE INFERENCE	MEAN INFERENCE (POSSIBLY THE TRUTH)
how **many** minutes?	10 - 30	120+
the **meaning** of 'own'	PAID FOR MOST OF IT	HEAVILY MORTGAGED

4. "Earn up to $500 a week in your spare time."

WHAT DID YOU INFER ABOUT —	NICE INFERENCE	MEAN INFERENCE (POSSIBLY THE TRUTH)
the **amount** most people can earn?	$300 - $500	$50 - $100
the **number** of hours of spare time?	10 - 20 HOURS	60 + HOURS
how **much** you have to spend on expenses?	VERY LITTLE	MOST MONEY EARNED

5. "This car (Brand X) will go further on a tank of petrol/gasoline."

WHAT DID YOU INFER ABOUT —	NICE INFERENCE	MEAN INFERENCE (POSSIBLY THE TRUTH)
the **size** of the tank compared with other cars?	SAME SIZE TANK	MUCH LARGER TANK THAN MOST CARS

6. "Smoke Drago cigarettes. World's finest. Guaranteed to please. Welcome to Drago Country."

WHAT DID YOU INFER ABOUT —	NICE INFERENCE	MEAN INFERENCE (POSSIBLY THE TRUTH)
World's finest **what**?	CIGARETTES	LUNG DESTROYERS
who they will please?	THE SMOKER	THE UNDERTAKER
the **location** of Drago Country?	PRETTY OUTDOORS PLACE	THE CEMETERY

23.   GENERALIZING

Generalizations are conclusions we make after observing quite a few particular examples or cases of something. Because we may not have observed all of the examples of a particular thing, our generalizations may be incorrect. Consequently, we modify our generalizations as we see future examples that don't fit our generalizations.

It is important to continually make generalizations as they help us link new observations and information to information already stored in our brains. Generalizations make it easier for us to store information and to remember and understand information.

Consider the following example

Jill finds the following shapes in the math room. All are labeled "triangle."

Jill generalizes that —
   "a triangle is a closed, 2 dimensional figure that has 3 sides and 3 angles."

If in future Jill observes a figure with these features she knows it is a triangle.

LOOK CAREFULLY AT THE INFORMATION GIVEN IN THE FOLLOWING EXAMPLES. SEE IF YOU CAN SEE ANY PATTERNS OR COMMON FEATURES IN THE SEPARATE THINGS GIVEN IN EACH EXAMPLE. THEN WRITE DOWN ALL THE GENERALIZATIONS YOU CAN MAKE FROM THE THINGS GIVEN IN EACH EXAMPLE.

EXAMPLES	**GENERALIZATIONS**

Here are some examples from **Mathematics and Language Arts**

1.   Here are some **quadilaterals**

QUADRILATERALS ARE 2D, CLOSED

FIGURES WITH FOUR SIDES

2. Here are some **perfect squares**

   25, 9, 49, 191

   If you find out that 4 is a perfect square, do you need to change your generalization?

   PERFECT SQUARES ARE FORMED BY MULTIPLYING A NUMBER BY ITSELF

3. Here are some **pronouns**.

   I, he, she, we, they

   PRONOUNS ARE WORDS USED TO DESCRIBE PEOPLE

4. Here are some **polygons**.

   POLYGONS ARE 2D CLOSED FIGURES WITH THREE OR MORE SIDES

5. Here are some **inanimate** things.

   rocks, fences, roads, sand, pencil, chair

   INANIMATE THINGS ARE LIFELESS.

Here are some examples from **Science**

6. Here are some *formulae* for **organic substances**

   CH_a, CH_3OH, $H.COOH$, C_2H_4.

   If you found an organic substance with a formula $CH_3. NH_2$ would you change your generalization?

   THE FORMULA OF ORGANIC SUBSTANCES CONTAIN C (CARBON) AND H (HYDROGEN)

   NO

7. Here are some bugs an astronaut finds on a planet. What generalization can she make about the bugs she finds?

   THE BUGS ON THE PLANET HAVE 2 STRIPES ON THEIR BODY

   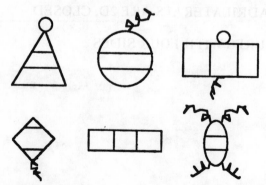

   On another visit she finds a new bug, shown here.

   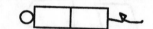

   Does she have to change her generalization?

   YES, AT LEAST ONE STRIPE

8. Jack looks through his microscope and sees the following ZETAS

What can Jack generalize about a ZETA?

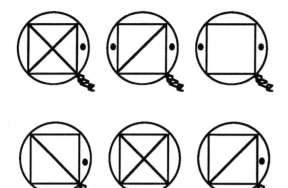

A ZETA IS CIRCULAR IN THE BODY

WITH A FOUR SIDED SHAPE INSIDE

9.

BIRDS	WARM BLOODED?	EAT?	FLY?	LAY EGGS?	LEGS?	WINGS?	BEAK?
emu	yes	seeds	no	yes	2	2	yes
eagle	yes	meat	yes	yes	2	2	yes
robin	yes	seeds	yes	yes	2	2	yes
sparrow	yes	seeds	yes	yes	2	2	yes
owl	yes	meat	yes	yes	2	2	yes

GENERALIZATION:

A BIRD IS A WARM-BLOODED ANIMAL WITH TWO WINGS, TWO LEGS AND A BEAK. IT LAYS EGGS.

10.

SUBSTANCE	CONDUCTS ELECTRICITY	TEMPERATURE MELTS AT	STATE	ATTRACTED BY MAGNET
iron	yes	high	solid	yes
plastic	no	low	solid	no
copper	yes	medium	solid	no
butter	no	low	solid	no
aluminium	yes	medium	solid	no
glass	no	high	solid	no
tin	yes	low	solid	no

GENERALIZATIONS: METALS ARE SOLIDS THAT CONDUCT ELECTRICITY

Here are some examples from **Social Studies**

11. PRESIDENT OF USA	AGE WHEN ELECTED	AGE AT DEATH	PREVIOUS OCCUPATION	STATE BORN IN	POLITICAL PARTY
Abraham Lincoln	52	56	Lawyer	Kentucky	Republican
William Taft	51	72	Lawyer	Ohio	Republican
Herbert Hoover	54	90	Engineer	Iowa	Republican
Franklin Roosevelt	51	63	Lawyer	New York	Democrat
William McKinley	54	58	Lawyer	Ohio	Republican
Grover Cleveland	55	71	Lawyer	New Jersey	Democrat
James Buchanan	65	77	Lawyer	Pennsylvania	Democrat

GENERALIZATIONS: AMERICAN PRESIDENTS ARE MEN, AT LEAST 50 YEARS OF AGE, WHO ARE LAWYERS. THEY ARE EITHER REPUBLICANS OR DEMOCRATS FROM THE EAST COAST.

12. **AVERAGE NUMBER OF DAYS OF PRECIPITATION (RAIN OR SNOW)**

* Top Figure **Winter** (December, January, February)
Bottom Figure **Summer** (June, July, August)

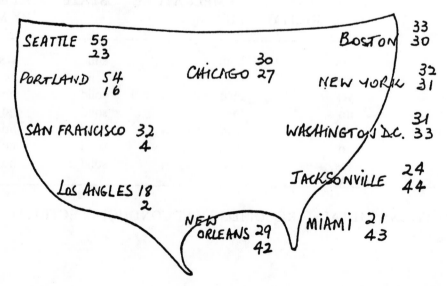

GENERALIZATIONS

1. AMERICAN CITIES ON THE WEST COAST HAVE MORE PRECIPITATION IN THE WINTER THAN THEY DO IN SUMMER.

2. AMERICAN CITIES IN THE NORTHEAST HAVE ABOUT THE SAME AMOUNT OF PRECIPITATION IN SUMMER AND WINTER.

3. AMERICAN CITIES IN THE SOUTHEAST HAVE MORE PRECIPITATION IN SUMMER THAN THEY DO IN THE WINTER.

24.   THINKING FLEXIBLY ABOUT PROBLEMS

People who are good at solving problems in school and out of school are flexible thinkers. They generally do the following things to help them.

1)   **become clear** as to **what is given** and what they have **to solve**.

2)   **picture** the problem so that it is not simply many meaningless words.

Well here are some tips from good problem solvers. Use them where you can to solve the following problems. When the class has had a chance to solve them, listen carefully to the thoughts of students who did have success. The teacher should ask a successful student to talk out loud, slowly and carefully, exactly what went through his or her mind as the problem was tackled.

GOOD PROBLEM SOLVERS

1)   UNDERLINE important given things to use or do.

2)   TALK OUT LOUD to themselves as they read the given information, sketch it on paper, and try different things.

3)   SKETCH diagrams, tables, graphs, concept maps and so on to summarize the information.

4)   SIMPLIFY problems by trying simpler numbers or things to see how a similar but simpler problem can be solved.

5)   BREAK problems up into small pieces that can be solved bit by bit.

6)   SHUT their eyes to help draw a mental picture or image of the given pieces of information.

TRY TO SOLVE THE FOLLOWING PROBLEMS BY USING AS MANY OF THE ABOVE SIX TIPS FOR SOLVING PROBLEMS AS YOU CAN.

---

1.   How would you get a ping pong ball out of a pipe that is 10 inches (25 cms) long and just wider than the ball. One end of the pipe is stuck in concrete. You are not allowed to damage the pipe, the ball, or the concrete.

FILL PIPE WITH WATER, USE A VACUUM CLEANER, GUM ON THE END OF A STICK.

2.   There is a circular pond full of water.
There is a big rock in the middle exactly 5 meters from all edges of the pond.
You have two planks of wood each 4½ meters long.

You have nothing to join the planks together with.
How can you get out to the rock without getting wet?

PLACE PLANKS AT RIGHT ANGLES

3. You have dropped a metal iron key down a narrow, 40 inch (100 cms) deep hold in the ground.
    How can you recover your key?

A HOOK ON A STRING, A MAGNET ON A STRING, SOME GUM ON THE END OF A STICK.

4. You are in the kitchen.
    You can't get the screw top off a cola bottle with your fingers.
    You don't have any tools handy.
    What are some ways you might screw the top off?
    What's in the kitchen that can grip the top more tightly than your fingers?

PLACE THE TOP IN THE GAP NEAR THE HINGES OF AN OPEN DOOR.
CLOSE THE DOOR TO JAM THE TOP. TURN THE BOTTLE.

25.   DEFINING MATHEMATICS PROBLEMS WITH SKETCHES

Drawing a sketch or diagram of the given things in a problem can often help you solve the problem.

Words and more words in a problem can be hard to picture in your mind.

This exercise uses some **line and table sketches** to help solve some math problems.

EXAMPLES:

Dick is shorter than Mary. Mary is shorter than Jan. Jan is taller than Phil. Phil is shorter than Dick. Who is the shortest person?

---

1.   First draw in a line. Lable one end Short (S) and the other end tall (T)

SHORT (S) _____ TALL (T)

2.   Now mark in the given facts one at a time.

Dick   Mary

1)   S _____ T   "Mary is shorter than Jan"

3)   Not sure where Phil is.

4)   Phil   Dick   Mary   Jan

      S _____ T   "Phil is shorter than Dick

SOLUTION: The shortest person is Phil.

SOLVE THE FOLLOWING PROBLEMS BY USING A LINE WITH LABELS AT EACH END.

---

1.   David is taller than Fred.
      George is not as tall as Fred.
      David is not as tall as Gary.
      Who is the shortest?

GEORGE

76

2.   John is older than Sam but younger than Len.
     Jack is younger than all three.
     Who is second oldest?

                            JOHN

3.   Mary runs further than anyone.
     Oscar doesn't run as far as Fred.
     Scott runs further than Fred but not as far as Jane.
     Who runs the least distance?

                            OSCAR

4.   Jill was born 2 years after Pam.
     Rita is 4 years older than Jill.
     Jean is 8 years younger than Rita.
     Tess was born a little after Jean.
     Who is the second oldest girl?
     You might use a number or age line here.

                            JILL

Now here is a problem that is helped with a table.

TOM, GEOFF, JANE AND MARG ALL LIKE DIFFERENT PETS. ONE
LIKES CATS, ONE LIKES DOGS, ONE LIKES HORSES, AND THE
OTHER PREFERS BIRDS. FIND OUT THE PET EACH PERSON
PREFERS.

Here we have TWO sets of variables.

   1)   different people
   2)   different pets

Rather than use a labelled line we need a labelled table.

	CATS	DOGS	HORSES	BIRDS
TOM				
GEOFF				
JANE				
MARG				

We still can't solve the problem without some clues

Clues

1. Jane is frightened of dogs.
2. Geoff has a saddle.
3. Tom buys seed for his pet.

Place the names in a column down the page. Place preferences of these people in columns across the top of the page.

e.g.

✓ likes
X doesn't like

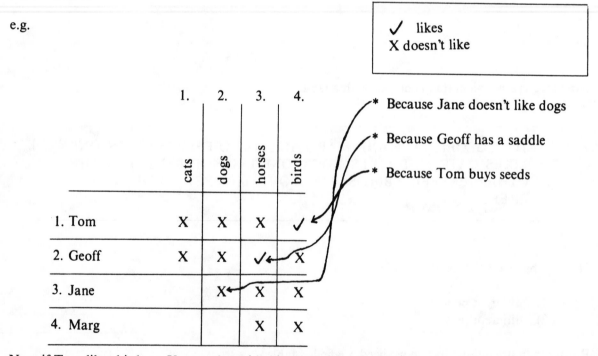

* Because Jane doesn't like dogs

* Because Geoff has a saddle

* Because Tom buys seeds

Now if Tom likes birds an X goes alongside his name for other pets (horizontal row 1).
    if Geoff likes horses an X goes alongside his name for other pets (horizontal row 2).
    if Tom likes birds an X goes under birds for the other people (vertical row 4).
    if Geoff likes horses an X goes under horses for the other people (verticle row 3).

Jane must like cats as she dislikes the other animals. (horizontal row 3).
Therefore, Marg must like dogs.

EXERCISES

(1) Bill, Mike, Mary and Alan all love sports and games.
     One loves water sports, another is good at board games, one loves ball games and the
     other loves gymnastics.
     Find out the sport or game each prefers.

     Clues
     1. Mary loves gymnastics but not water sports.
     2. Alan and Mary get bored with board games.
     3. Bill is a great chess player.
     4. Mike thinks ball games are dangerous.

     **MARY PREFERS GYM, MIKE WATER SPORTS, BILL BOARD GAMES,
     ALAN BALL GAMES**

(2) Tom, Dick, Jan, Tina and Scott each love a special color: No two of them like the same color.
     Which color does each of them prefer?

     Clues
     1. Tom's favorite is **not** red.
     2. Dick hates both red and blue.
     3. Jan likes yellow.
     4. Tina can't stand orange.
     5. Scott really likes orange.
     6. Someone likes green.

     **TOM LOVES BLUE, DICK — GREEN, JANE — YELLOW, TINA — RED,
     SCOTT — ORANGE**

(3) Jill, Bev, and Eve play in the school hockey team. One is center forward, another is center
     halfback and the other the goalkeeper.

     Jill and the goalkeeper celebrated Eve's birthday with her.

     Jill is not the center halfback.

     What position does each girl play?

     JILL — CENTER FORWARD, BEV — GOALKEEPER, EVE — CENTER BACK

(4) Geoff, Ned and Sam are either an accountant, a computer programmer or a music teacher.
     Geoff is not an accountant or computer programmer.
     Ned is not an accountant.
     What are their jobs?

     GEOFF — MUSIC TEACHER, NED — COMPUTERS, SAM — ACCOUNTANT

(5) Jill, Kit and Lisa have either $1, $3, or $10 each.
Lisa has the most money.
Lisa and Jill have more than $1 each.
How much does each have?

JILL $3, KIT $1, LISA $10

EVALUATING SKILLS

Exercises 26-33 aim to help you evaluate how accurate, relevant, truthful, biased and reasonable information is.

The skills include —

Establishing criteria — setting criteria for making judgements.

Verifying — helping to confirm the accuracy of information.

Identifying errors — in relevance, truth and other characteristics.

26. IDENTIFYING ERRORS 1. — FACTS FROM OPINIONS

Facts are quite different from opinions. Each day you will hear on T.V. and radio or you will read in newspapers and magazines, statements made by people. Some of the statements made appear as though they are facts. However, in many cases these 'facts' are only the opinions of the people who make the statements.

The exercises below will help you recognize the difference between a fact and an opinion. If you have this thinking skill, your pool of knowledge will be more valid and accurate. You won't be misled by statements that appear to be facts but in reality are only opinions.

Here is a check list of the features of facts as against opinions. Use them to identify whether any statement you hear or read is a fact or an opinion.

FACTS	OPINIONS
• actually happened or existed in the past.	• possibly will happen in the future (or happened in the past).
• very few people will disagree with statements of facts.	• quite a few people may disagree with statements of opinions.
• involve numerical information or specific instances.	• general statements not actually proven.
• based on the experiences of many people.	• based on what an individual believes, feels, or guesses is probably true.

EXAMPLES

Facts

1. Insects have six legs.

2. Food is a basic human need.

Opinions

1. Algebra is a more difficult subject than Geometry.

2. Cotton is a more useful fiber than wool.

IN THE BRACKETS AFTER EACH STATEMENT MARK AN (F) IF YOU THINK IT IS A FACT, OR AN (O) IF YOU THINK IT IS AN OPINION. USE THE CRITERIA GIVEN IN THE EXPLANATION.

Here are some examples from **Mathematics, Language Arts, Science** and **Social Studies**

1. There are more nouns in a language than there are verbs   (F)

2. Percentages are more useful than fractions   (O)

3. Girls are better at reading than boys   (O)

4. An acute angle is smaller than an obtuse angle   (F)

5. Mathematics is more difficult than History   (O)

6. Insects always have six legs   (F)

7. All insects are harmful   (O)

8. The sun is larger than the moon   (F)

9. The sun is more important than the moon for allowing life on earth   (F)

10. Dogs make better pets than cats   (O)

11. The President of the U.S.A. has always been a man   (F)

12. The President of the U.S.A. should always be a man   (O)

13. Women can't handle stress as well as men   (O)

14. Women tend to live longer than men   (F)

15. Producing electricity from uranium is more harmful to humans than producing it from coal   (O)

16. More ultra violet light is reaching the earth from the sun than it did ten years ago   (F)

Articles you read in magazines or in newspapers usually contain a **mixture** of **facts** and **opinions**.

You should always be on your guard as to what is a fact and what is an opinion. You can trust facts. However, you can't be sure whether opinions are true or correct.

Unfortunately, clever writers mislead people by stating opinions rather than facts about things these people are interested in.

THE FOLLOWING ARTICLES CONTAIN A MIXTURE OF FACTS AND OPINIONS. AN ARROW POINTS TO THESE FACTS OR OPINIONS. THINK ABOUT THE FEATURES OF A FACT AND AN OPINION. NOW WRITE IN THE WORD **FACT** OR **OPINION** AT THE END OF THE ARROW TO SHOW WHETHER A SENTENCE IS A FACT OR AN OPINION.

ALSO MAKE UP A HEADING TO SHOW THE MAIN IDEA OF THE ARTICLE.

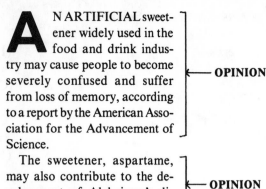

AN ARTIFICIAL sweetener widely used in the food and drink industry may cause people to become severely confused and suffer from loss of memory, according to a report by the American Association for the Advancement of Science. — **OPINION**

The sweetener, aspartame, may also contribute to the development of Alzheimer's disease, the conference was told. — **OPINION**

According to Dr. H.J. Roberts, director of the Palm Beach Institute for Medical Research in Florida, the sweetener is marketed widely as NutraSweet in the US. — **FACT**

He believed the effects of aspartame "posed an imminent health hazard and should be investigated as soon as possible." — **OPINION**

He said more than 100m people consumed products containing the substance. — **FACT**

Aspartame was first synthesized in Japan. It is 200 times sweeter than sugar and breaks down into phenylalanine, aspartic acic and methyl alcohol. — **FACT**

Dr. Roberts studied a group of 551 people who reacted to aspartame and found severe problems arose in 28.5 p.c.

Some lost vision in one or both eyes and about a third suffered from severe dizziness.

Dr. Roberts said an 18-year-old who daily drank two litres of soft drink containing the sweetener could not at times find his way home when driving in his own neighborhood. — **FACT**

One woman who had been free of seizures for a year went into convulsions five minutes after chewing gum flavored with aspartame.

He says excessive amounts of phenylalanine, an essential amino acid, affects the brain and nervous system.

WASHINGTON — When you shiver from the cold, be grateful—it could save your life. That's the conclusion of Gordon Giesbrecht, a Canadian scientist — **OPINION** who immersed himself and five other volunteers in iced water to study the effects on the human body of extreme cold. — **FACT**

What he found is that the body's natural shiver may be more warming than hot-water bottles or exercise for a person caught outside in severe cold. — **OPINION**

"Shivering warms the body," Giesbrecht said. "Making the heat is the only reason you shiver in the first place. That's been known for a long time."

But Giesbrecht learned from his study that warmth from an external source for a person suffering from moderate hypothermia, or body chill, may actually be harmful because it stops the natural shivering reflex.

NEW YORK — Doctors claim they have developed a new blood test that can identify alcoholics, even when they have not had a drink for several years.

The doctors say the test could become an important means of spotting alcoholism early so it can be treated before permanent damage occurs. — **OPINION**

They also believe it may even give them a way to identify children who are at high risk of becoming alcoholics as adults.

The researchers, from several US institutes, say their test is about 75 p.c. accurate in distinguishing alcoholics from people who do not have drinking problems.

The test measures the activity of two chemicals produced by platelets, the blood cells responsible for clotting. The substances are enzymes called monoamine oxidase and adenylate cyclase. — **FACT**

The researchers say they found that the activity of the two enzymes was significantly reduced in alcoholics. — **FACT**

27.   IDENTIFYING ERRORS 2. — POOR REASONING

Reasoning involves the drawing of conclusions from some evidence that we have. Frequently people show poor reasoning by "jumping" to conclusions. In other words they make a conclusion based on one or more poor assumptions.

For example we can assume —

    A.   that a whole thing has the same properties as each of its individual parts.

        e.g.   Mary is very clever at English. Her English class must be outstanding.

    B.   that an individual or special case has the same properties as the large group of things that the individual belongs to.

        e.g.   Most bears are dangerous, therefore we should avoid Koala bears.

    C.   that something happened only because some other things happened before it.

        e.g.   If Mr. Whittle hadn't invented the jet engine, we would not have jet planes today.

    D.   that one particular property automatically follows from the existence of another property.

        e.g.   All homes in Green Hills are expensive, therefore they must be well built.

READ EACH OF THE FOLLOWING POOR REASONS CAREFULLY.
INDICATE WHICH OF THE ABOVE TYPES OF ASSUMPTIONS (A, B, C OR D) ARE BEING MADE IN EACH REASON.
THEN THINK UP AND WRITE DOWN YOUR OWN EXAMPLES OF POOR REASONING.
GIVE ONE OR TWO EXAMPLES FOR EACH OF THE FOUR TYPES OF ASSUMPTION GIVEN HERE.)

---

1.   If Albert Einstein hadn't been born, there would not be any atom bombs in the world today.

ASSUMPTION: TYPE: C

MY SIMILAR EXAMPLE: IF MARY HAD WORN HER SHOES, SHE WOULD NOT HAVE TWISTED HER ANKLE.

2.   In general, fruits have seeds inside of them. Strawberries have seeds on the outside. Therefore strawberries can't be fruits.

ASSUMPTION: TYPE: B

MY SIMILAR EXAMPLE: SPANISH PEOPLE HAVE BLACK HAIR. MARIO HAS BLACK HAIR, THEREFORE MARIO IS SPANISH.

3. The parts of this computer are very inexpensive, therefore the computer will be very inexpensive.

ASSUMPTION: TYPE: A

MY SIMILAR EXAMPLE: MICK THE GREEK IS VERY RICH. GREECE MUST BE A VERY WEALTHY COUNTRY.

4. Metals are generally shing solids. Therefore the metal mercury must be a solid.

ASSUMPTION: TYPE: B

MY SIMILAR EXAMPLE: THE CHINESE ARE GOOD AT GYMNASTICS. THE CHINESE STUDENT WILL BE GOOD AT THE PARALLEL BARS.

5. This poem is very short, so it can't be very interesting.

ASSUMPTION: TYPE: D

MY SIMILAR EXAMPLE: THE ELEPHANT IS VERY HEAVY SO IT WILL SINK IN WATER.

6. Aluminum is very light, so it can't be very strong.

ASSUMPTION: TYPE: D

MY SIMILAR EXAMPLE: TOM DOESN'T VISIT THE LIBRARY, HE MUSTN'T LIKE READING.

7. If Bill hadn't come to school today he would not have broken his wrist.

ASSUMPTION: TYPE: C

MY SIMILAR EXAMPLE: IF HELEN HAD GONE TO BED EARLY, OUR TEAM WOULD HAVE WON THE COMPETITION.

28.   IDENTIFYING ERRORS 3. — RELEVANCE OF INFORMATION

Write down what you think the meaning of relevant is. Compare your definition with that given by others in the class and check it with a dictionary definition.

Information is relevant if it helps to explain or clarify.
Relevant information helps understanding and is connected with the topic being considered.

Now, not all the information we read, hear, or write ourselves is relevant. 'Padding' or irrelevant information, can often confuse and mislead the reader. We have to learn to sort out what is relevant and what is not relevant.

If we learn to focus on what is helpful or relevant we will communicate more clearly, make better decisions, and solve problems more easily.

SEE IF YOU CAN IDENTIFY OR PROVIDE THE RELEVANT INFORMA-
TION IN THE FOLLOWING SITUATIONS.
PLACE A TICK (√) IN THE BRACKETS IF RELEVANT AND A CROSS (X) IN
THE BRACKETS IF IRRELEVANT.

---

1. You are very keen to buy a breakfast cereal that is good for your health. Which of the following things written on a cereal box are relevant when making your choice?

   1) It tastes good   (√)
   2) It contains high fiber   (√)
   3) Iron Man eats it   (X)
   4) It doesn't have many calories   (√)
   5) The company sponsors the Olympics   (X)
   6) It contains no preservatives   (√)

2. Jack wants to borrow a library book to help him with his project about football. Which of the following features of the book would be helpful or of little help to a librarian trying to find a suitable book for Jack? Mark the helpful characteristics with a (√) and the unhelpful with a (X).

   The book I want must be . . .
   1) inexpensive   (X)
   2) about football   (√)
   3) suitable for a grade 4 to 7 student   (√)
   4) written in the last 5 years   (√)
   5) covered with a hard cover   (X)
   6) more than 2 centimeters thick   (X)

3. Mary lost her pet dog and wants to place an advertisement in the paper under the lost property column. Place a (√) by those things on her list that will be useful in finding her dog. Place an (X) by any unhelpful or irrelevant things.

    My dog

    1. is black   (√)
    2. was a birthday present   (X)
    3. is about 24 cms high   (√)
    4. is a good sleeper at night   (X)
    5. has a short tail   (√)
    6. hates my neighbor's dog   (X)
    7. answers to the name of 'Blackey' (X)

---

4. You want to apply for an after school job at the supermarket. The manager asks you to write down some things about yourself that might help you get the job. Which of the following things about yourself would NOT be relevant or helpful for the manager? Mark them with a cross (X).

    I am...

    1. 15 years of age   ( )
    2. left handed   (X)
    3. good at arithmetic   ( )
    4. a member of the school soccer team (X)
    5. a good bicycle rider   (X)
    6. very healthy and reliable   ( )

---

5. You want to sell your bike. List the details you would include on a notice to place in the newspaper or inside a local shop window?

---

6. Imagine that you have to interview six students for the job of delivering the evening newspaper in the neighborhood. Only one student can be selected. List some relevant questions you would ask them in order for you to make the best choice.

29. ESTABLISHING CRITERIA FOR DECISION MAKING

Making a decision involves making a choice from a range of suitable things or possibilities. Each choice usually has some good things about it as well as some poor things about it. For example, if you had to decide on a pet, a parrot might **be good** because it
1) is inexpensive to feed.
2) is easy to leave for a few days.
3) doesn't get sick very often.

The **bad things** about a parrot might be that
1) it can't be cuddled.
2) it makes a mess in its cage.

These things such as expense, ease of leaving, health and so on, are **relevant factors or criteria** we should consider in choosing a pet.

For each of these factors you can give the following points for the extent that they are present
e.g.   3 — factor is present to a high degree
        2— factor is present to an average degree
        1 — factor is present to a low degree

Let us try to give points for the above five factors when choosing between a parrot, a dog, and a rabbit.

	FACTORS	PARROT	DOG	RABBIT
1.	INEXPENSIVE TO FEED	3	1	3
2.	EASY TO LEAVE	2	1	3
3.	DOESN'T GET SICK	3	2	3
4.	CUDDLY	1	3	1
5.	NOT MESSY	1	3	1
	TOTALS	10	10	12

If this is how you score the choices you should decide on a rabbit! If deep down your really want a dog, then you will have to make one or more factors more important than the others. For example, if you think the factors of "cuddly" and "not messy" are twice as important as the other factors, you can multiply these points by 2. Now 3 points becomes 6 points, 2 points becomes 4 points, and 1 point becomes 2 points.

AS A CLASS THINK UP SOME FACTORS TO CONSIDER FOR THE FOLLOWING DECISIONS. DECIDE ON **FOUR** IMPORTANT FACTORS FOR EACH. WRITE THEM IN ON THE TABLES. NOW YOU PERSONALLY GIVE 1, 2, OR 3 POINTS FOR THE CHOICES GIVEN. WHAT ARE YOUR DECISIONS?

1. THE JOB I WOULD PREFER

1. FACTORS TO CONSIDER	TEACHER	DOCTOR	GARDENER	ROCK STAR
1. MUCH TRAVEL	1	1	1	3
2. WELL PAID	1	3	1	3
3. SECURE JOB	2	3	1	1
4. MEET MANY PEOPLE	3	3	1	3
TOTALS	7	10	4	10

2. THE COUNTRY I WOULD LIKE TO VISIT

FACTORS TO CONSIDER	CANADA	SWEDEN	IRAN	FIJI
1. CLOSE TO USA	3	2	1	1
2. LOW COST OF LIVING	2	2	3	2
3. GOOD POLITICAL STABILITY	3	3	1	1
4. ENGLISH SPEAKING	3	1	1	3
TOTALS	11	8	6	7

1. In the last exercise we saw that making a decision involves choosing between different possibilities.

Now let us imagine that you have to make a decision that affects other people. In this exercise you have to decide on the best place to set up a camp on an island.

Look carefully at the information given here. On the following table list the factors you would consider. Then give 3, 2 or 1 points for these factors considering the four places A, B, C and D on the island. Add up your totals. Where is the best location in your opinion?

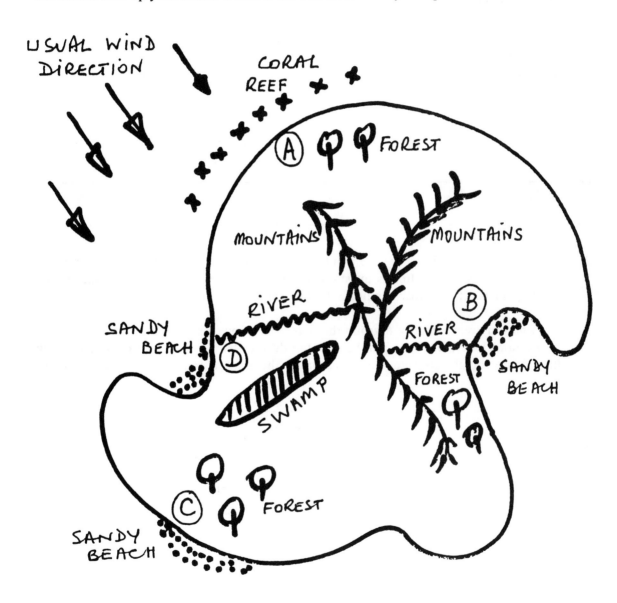

	FACTORS TO CONSIDER	A	B	PLACES ON ISLAND C	D
1.	WELL PROTECTED FROM WIND	1	3	1	1
2.	CLOSE TO SWIMMING BEACH	1	3	3	3
3.	NEAR FOREST FOR WOOD	3	1	3	1
4.	NEAR RIVER FOR WATER	1	3	1	3
5.					
6.					
	TOTALS	6	10	8	8

2. In the previous question you gave points or ratings to various factors that were important in deciding on a campsite. In this question you have to place in order of importance (or rank) various things. The number 1 indicates first in importance and so on.

Imagine you are a leader of a group that has been shipwrecked on an island. The island has bushes and bird life. Place numbers alongside the items you have salvaged to show the importance you give to them. Give a reason for the first few and last few items of importance.

ITEMS	ORDER OF IMPORTANCE	REASONS
matches	2	TO LIGHT FIRES FOR WARMTH
first aid kit		
life raft		
pistol/bullets	3	TO KILL BIRDS FOR FOOD
compass		

5 gallons of pure water	1	TO STOP DEHYDRATION
radio		
flares		
oxygen in cylinders	11	PLENTY OF OXYGEN IN AIR
50 metres of rope	10	
a sail		

3.   PROBLEM: Where is the best location to place a town dump for burning the town's rubbish?

   ALTERNATIVES: Locations A, B, C, D, E or F on the given map.

TOWN MAP

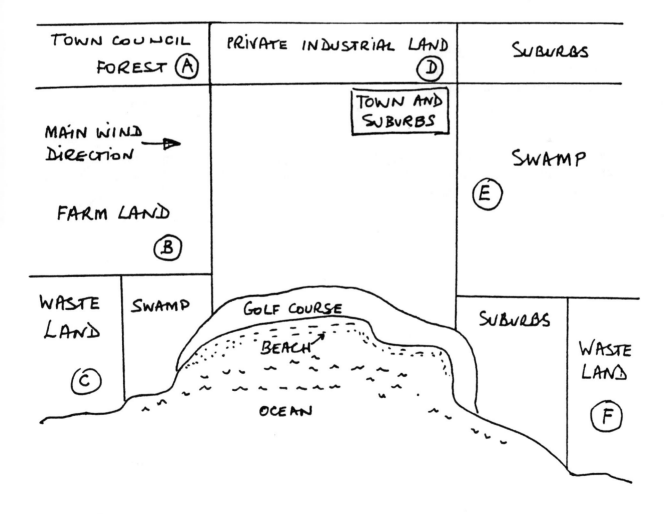

COMPLETE THE FOLLOWING TABLE. LIST OTHER RELEVANT FACTORS TO CONSIDER. OPPOSITE EACH FACTOR RATE THE LOCATIONS A 3, 2 OR 1 FOR THIS FACTOR. WHICH IS THE BEST LOCATION IN YOUR OPINION?

FACTORS TO CONSIDER	A	B	C	D	E	F
CLOSE TO CITY	2	2	1	3	2	1
CHEAP LAND	3	1	3	1	3	3
SMOKE WON'T PASS OVER SUBURBS	1	2	2	1	3	3
LOW EXPENSE TO PREPARE LAND	3	3	3	3	1	3
TOTALS	9	8	9	8	9	10

3 = factor present to a high degree
2 = factor present to a medium degree
1 = factor present to a low degree

4. Mary finds that her bedroom facing the western sun gets very hot in summer. List at least four things her parents could do to overcome this problem. Also list the advantages and disadvantages of each solution that you select.

	SOLUTIONS	ADVANTAGES	DISADVANTAGES
1.	AND AIRCONDITIONER IN HER BEDROOM	INSTALLATION QUICK EFFICIENT, CONTROLLED COOLING	HIGH COST NOISY CONTINUAL COST OF ELECTRICITY
2.	OUTSIDE WINDOW SHADING	INSTALLATION QUICK NO ONGOING COSTS FOR ELECTRICITY	MEDIUM COST SHADES WOULD CUT OUT VIEW SHADES WOULD CUT ANY BREEZE

3.	ERECTING A PERGOLA WITH SHADY VINE GROWING ON IT	IMPROVE APPEARANCE OF HOUSE VIEW FROM INSIDE BETTER VINE WOULD COOL AIR NO ONGOING COSTS	MEDIUM COST SEVERAL YEARS FOR VINE TO GROW NO LEAVES ON VINE NO SHADE
4.	PLANTING QUICK GROWING DECIDUOUS TREES OUTSIDE THE WINDOWS	LITTLE COST MAKE SHADE AND COOL AIR IMPROVE THE VIEW ENCOURAGE BIRDS	SEVERAL YEARS BEFORE SHADE AVAILABLE NO LEAVES — NO SHADE

31.   ESTABLISHING CRITERIA FOR FINDING A CAUSE

We have all thought about the **reason or cause** for something that has happened. It may have been the cause for —

- your bicycle tire going flat at school.

- the death of a bird you find out in the street.

- the family car not starting first thing in the morning.

- the extinction of the dinosaurs from the earth, and so on.

In looking for a cause you should

1. List all the **possible causes** regardless of how unlikely they may appear.

2. List all the **pieces of evidence** found around the place where something you are trying to explain has happened.

3. Use each piece of evidence to either support or reject each possible cause that you have listed.

Here is an example —

Your mother turns the key to start the car. The engine tries to start but it doesn't keep going. Use the three point system to find the cause for this event.

1. **Possible Causes**

   1) Flat battery.   4) Faulty key switch.
   2) Out of fuel.   5) Carburettor blocked.
   3) Battery cable loose.   6) Engine frozen with ice.

2. **Evidence collected**

   A) All cables tight.
   B) Fuel gauge shows half full.
   C) Lights turn on brightly.
   D) The morning temperature is 70° F.
   E) Engine partly turns over.

3.

POSSIBLE CAUSES	EVIDENCE COLLECTED				
	A	B	C	D	E
1. Flat battery			X		
2. Out of fuel		X			
3. Cable loose	X				
4. Faulty key switch					
5. Carburetor blocked					X
6. Engine 'iced'				X	

X = evidence shows that this **is not** the cause.

On the table above the column A an (X) is placed opposite "loose cable". Evidence A is that all cables are tight. In column B an (X) is placed opposite "out of fuel". Evidence B is that the "fuel gauge shows half full". In column C an (X) is placed opposite "flat battery" because the evidence C — "the lights turn on" indicates that the cause can't be a flat battery. In column D an (X) is placed opposite "engine iced" as the evidence "it is 70° F" rules this out as the reason. In column E an (X) is placed opposite "faulty switch" as the evidence that the engine turns over rules this cause out.

The only cause listed without any (X)'s opposite it is "carburettor blocked". This must be the best explanation from the evidence found.

IN THE FOLLOWING EXERCISE FIRST BRAINSTORM OR LIST ANY POSSIBLE CAUSES FOR EACH EVENT. WHEN YOU HAVE DONE THIS, READ THE GIVEN FACTS AND LIST ANY RELEVANT EVIDENCE. COMPLETE THE TABLE AS SHOWN IN THE EXAMPLE IN ORDER TO FIND THE MOST LIKELY CAUSE.

---

1. Your bicycle tire is flat when you come to ride it home from school. At this point list all usual and unusual causes in the spaces below.

POSSIBLE CAUSES

1. **PUNCTURED WITH NAIL**	4. **TIRE CUT BY GLASS**
2. **SOMEONE LET AIR OUT**	5.
3. **SUN CAUSED PATCH TO LIFT**	6.

Now read the facts and list any relevant evidence in the spaces below.

FACTS

It is unusual to find your back tire flat on the first Monday of the term. The bicycle was wet as it had been raining all day. There were no marks on the tire and no nails or sharp objects in it. The front tire was not flat but was covered with mud. Several other bicycles nearby also had flat tires.

EVIDENCE FOUND

A. **NO SUNSHINE AS RAINING ALL DAY**

B. **NO CUT MARKS ON TIRE**

C. **NO SHARP OBJECTS IN TIRE**

D.

E.

POSSIBLE CAUSES		EVIDENCE COLLECTED				
	A	B	C	D	E
1. PUNCTURED			X			
2. SOMEONE LET AIR OUT	MOST LIKELY CAUSE					
3. SUN CAUSED PATCH TO LIFT	X					
4. TIRE CUT BY GLASS		X				
5.						

2. When you cme to school on Monday you find the goldfish in your classroom aquarium are all dead. At this point list all usual and unusual causes in the spaces below.

POSSIBLE CAUSES

1. **POISONED BY SOMEONE**   4. **OLD AGE**

2. **DIED OF HUNGER**   5. **POKED BY SOMEONE**

3. **LACK OF OXYGEN**   6.

Now read the facts and list any relevant evidence in the spaces below.

FACTS

The aquarium was full of clear water. All of the fish were small and had been recently bought from Joe's Indoor Fish Shop. The engine of the aerator was still giving a steady stream of air bubbles to the water. The fish were floating on top of the water. There were no marks on any of the fish. A funny smell was present which could have come from the fish food floating on the water.

EVIDENCE FOUND

A. **SMALL (YOUNG) FISH**

B. **AIR BUBBLES IN AQUARIUM**

C. **FISH NOT MARKED**

D. **FOOD PRESENT**

E. **FUNNY SMELL PRESENT**

POSSIBLE CAUSES	EVIDENCE COLLECTED				
	A	B	C	D	E
1. POISONED	MOST LIKELY CAUSE				
2. DIED OF HUNGER				X	
3. LACK OF OXYGEN		X			
4. OLD AGE	X				
5. POKED BY SOMEONE			X		

POISONING THE MOST LIKELY CAUSE. THE SMELL IS IRRELEVANT — COULD BE DUE TO DEAD BODIES.

3. On your way to school you find a dead bird in the middle of your driveway. At this point list all usual and unusual causes in the spaces below.

POSSIBLE CAUSES

1. **POISONED**

2. **OLD AGE**

3. **FLEW INTO OBJECT**

4. **THIRST**

5. **SHOT BY SOMEONE**

6.

Now read the facts and list any relevant evidence in the spaces below.

FACTS

It has rained all night but the young bird looked healthy and plump. No blood could be found on the bird's feathers. The postman stopped to look at you pick up the bird. The neighbor's dog barked loudly as you took the bird inside. All you could find was a bruise on the bird's neck.

EVIDENCE FOUND

A. **BIRD HEALTHY AND PLUMP**

B. **NO BLOOD ON FEATHERS**

C. **BRUISE ON HEAD**

D. **WET NIGHT**

E. **YOUNG BIRD**

POSSIBLE CAUSES	EVIDENCE COLLECTED				
	A	B	C	D	E
1. POISONED	X				
2. OLD AGE					X
3. FLEW INTO OBJECT	MOST LIKELY CAUSE				
4. THIRST				X	
5. SHOT		X			

MOST LIKELY FLEW INTO A GLASS WINDOW OR A HEAVY OBJECT, SUCH AS A CAR.

32. VERIFYING THE ACCURACY OF SOMEONE'S CLAIM

Almost every day we read how someone claims to have seen an unidentifed flying object, a monster in a lake, a ghost in their room, or a strange kind of creature.

Next time you hear of or read about such a claim check it out by answering the questions on the following checklist with a yes or a no. In this way you have a better chance of systematically judging the accuracy, the truth and consistency of such a claim.

EXAMPLE

IMAGINE SOMEONE CLAIMS TO HAVE SEEN AN ANIMAL THAT SCIENTISTS BELIEVE HAS BEEN EXTINCT FOR MANY YEARS.

Here is our checklist of questions you could ask yourself. A (X) indicates that this is the answer to the question.

	QUESTION	Yes	No	Not sure
1.	Did the person see the thing first hand?	X		
2.	Did anyone else see what the person claims to have seen?		X	
3.	If so, is this person a reliable person?	X		
4.	Was the person experienced/trained at looking for such things?	X		
5.	Did the person use accurate equipment to make the observation?		X	
6.	Was the person wide awake, and not affected by drugs or alcohol?	X		
7.	Has the person written or spoken about such a thing before?	X		

QUESTION	Yes	No	Not sure
8. Did the person write up an account of what was seen immediately after seeing it?			X
9. Does the person look for publicity or money in making such observations?	X		
10. Does the person have a good reputation amongst his/her friends and fellow workers?	X		
11. Were the conditions good for viewing at the time the observation was made?		X	
12. Was the person possibly influenced by similar recent sightings made by other people?			X

The points in favor of believing the claims are —

The person was an experienced observer, wide awake and well thought of by friends and fellow workers.

The points against believing the claim are —

Only person to see thing, poor viewing conditions with no equipment used, emotionally involved in subject through previous writing and seeking publicity.

With this evidence for and against listed you have to make the judgement whether to believe or not.

In this case the evidence for disbelieving is probably stronger.

READ THE FOLLOWING CLAIMS MADE BY PEOPLE. USE YOUR CHECK-LIST TO ANSWER YES/NO/UNSURE TO EACH QUESTION ON THE LIST. SUMMARIZE YOUR ANSWERS TO THESE QUESTIONS. FINALLY, WRITE DOWN WHETHER YOU BELIEVE OR DISBELIEVE EACH CLAIM. GIVE REASONS FOR YOUR BELIEF.

---

1. Ann Thomas reported to the morning paper that she had observed an unknown comet. As a long time member of the national astronomy association she had made the observation with the association's latest electronic, laser telescope. Another member of an interstate astronomy association supported her claim by viewing the comet the next evening at the co-ordinates in the heavens that she reported.

   Do or don't you believe the claim? Why?

REASONS FOR BELIEVING CLAIM: ANN SAW FIRST HAND, ANOTHER RELIABLE PERSON SAW THE COMET NEXT EVENING. SHE IS A TRAINED OBSERVER, ACCURATE EQUIPMENT WAS USED.

REASONS FOR NOT BELIEVING CLAIM: THE OTHER OBSERVER COULD BE A FRIEND AND IMAGINED SIGHTING.

2. In 1960 Tor MacLeod claimed that he saw the Lock Ness Monster through his binoculars. The large grey, black mass was about a mile away on the opposite shore of the loch. It had elephant like trunks at the front and a square ended flipper on the back. MacLeod had moved to the area to live because he wanted to view the monster before he died of cancer. He viewed the monster for about eight minutes. The weather was dull and overcast with a drizzle of rain on the loch. MacLeod later told a friend, Ms. Whyte about the sighting, who then wrote about it in a book. The story of the monster basking in the sunshine was very believeable.

REASONS FOR BELIEVING CLAIM: USED EQUIPMENT TO VIEW THE MONSTER, VIEWING LASTED 8 MINUTES.

REASONS FOR NOT BELIEVING CLAIM: MONSTER LONG DISTANCE AWAY, MACLEOD DESPERATE TO SEE MONSTER, POOR VIEWING CONDITIONS, SOUGHT IMMEDIATE PUBLICITY, REPORT ON SUNSHINE NOT CONSISTENT WITH VIEWING CONDITIONS AT TIME OF SIGHTING. (OVERCAST/RAIN)

3. Over one thousand Americans have reported seeing Big Foot since 1818. Big Foot is reported to be a curious, gentle, eight foot beast, covered with 3″ of hair, and with a foot print about twice the size of a normal adult. Here is a typical report of a sighting.

    Jeff and Jim, two high school seniors, were driving around at night looking for Big Foot. One had been seen in the area the night before. Suddenly, they saw this monster smash down a wire fence in the dark. It approached their car. They saw two yellow glowing eyes about 100 feet away. The boys hit the monster with two gun shots. It didn't stop, but moved off in another direction making a giggling type of noise. The next morning they found no blood, but they found huge foot prints. They called the local newspaper to tell their story and to get the foot prints photographed. Their description of Big Foot was exactly the same as that of other people who had seen it the night before.

REASONS FOR BELIEVING CLAIM: 2 PEOPLE SAW BIG FOOT, VIEWING CLOSE TO BIG FOOT, FOOTPRINTS FOUND, DESCRIPTION MATCHES THAT OF OTHER PEOPLE.

REASONS FOR NOT BELIEVING CLAIM: INFLUENCED BY RECENT SIGHTINGS, SOUGHT IMMEDIATE PUBLICITY.

4. On November 2, 1957 in Levelland, Texas, twelve people claimed to have seen a flying saucer on the ground near their cars. The sightings were made within 3 hours from 11 o'clock at night until 2 o'clock in the morning. Two people saw a glowing yellow torpedo shaped object. The object caused their lights to go out and their engine to stop. One hour later another person had the same experience. Five minutes later, another person also had the same experience, which they described to the local radio station. All witnesses reported to the police, and all said the object was about 200 feet long and that a heavy mist and light rain was in the area. The Airforce said there was thunder and lightning in the area.

REASONS FOR BELIEVING CLAIM: MANY WITNESSES, SAUCER CLOSE, SAME DESCRIPTIONS OF SIGHTINGS.

REASONS FOR NOT BELIEVING CLAIM: SOUGHT PUBLICITY, INFLUENCED BY THE SIGHTINGS OF OTHERS, POOR VIEWING CONDITIONS.

33. IDENTIFYING ERRORS 4 — MISLEADING STATEMENTS

Advertising and newspaper headlines often use misleading statements to trap the unthinking reader. Be careful and don't be trapped by the following kinds of misleading statements.

A. Statements that **don't give any standard** or similar thing **to compare** the thing in the statement with.

    e.g.   Budget cars are **cheaper.**

B. Statements that **don't define the meaning** of key terms used in the statement.

    e.g.   **All cars** will be sold this weekend

C. Statements that make something unpleasant or undesireable sound more pleasant or desireable.

    e.g.   Say **farewell** nicely to your loved ones at Simplicity Funeral House.

D. Statements that use emotional words that appeal to your need for status, glamour, to be trendy, to have power and so on.

    e.g.   **Successful executives** are choosing QUICK calculators.

READ THE FOLLOWING STATEMENTS CAREFULLY, FOR EACH STATEMENT INDICATE WHETHER IT IS AN EXAMPLE OF AN A, B, C OR D TYPE STATEMENT. THEN WRITE IN WHAT YOU THINK THE UNDERLINED PART OF EACH STATEMENT COULD POSSIBLY MEAN.

FINALLY, TRY WRITING YOUR OWN STATEMENTS — ONE FOR EACH OF THE FOUR TYPES OF MISLEADING STATEMENTS GIVEN IN THIS EXERCISE. YOU MIGHT ALSO TRY TO FIND EXAMPLES OF THESE TYPES OF STATEMENTS IN MAGAZINES OR THE NEWSPAPER TO SHARE IN CLASS.

---

1. SHINO shines brighter!

    TYPE   STATEMENT:

    POSSIBLE MEANING: SHINO SHINES BRIGHTER THAN WATER/NOTHING. THE POOREST SHINE ON THE MARKET.

    MY SIMILAR EXAMPLE: PLYON THE PLASTIC PAINT, LASTS LONGER.

2. Sign up for a great career as a **sanitary engineer.**

   TYPE   STATEMENT:

   POSSIBLE MEANING: SIGN UP AS A GARBAGE COLLECTOR

   MY SIMILAR EXAMPLE: FRED IS FINDING IT DIFFICULT TO ADJUST TO CLASSROOM RULES.

3. Everything in the store goes at 50% off the **regular price.**

   TYPE   STATEMENT:

   POSSIBLE MEANING: EVERYTHING EQUALS THINGS THAT HAVEN'T SOLD LAST YEAR.
   REGULAR PRICE = MAXIMUM PRICE THINGS CAN BE SOLD AT.

   MY SIMILAR EXAMPLE: FOUR OUT OF FIVE PEOPLE PREFER EXACTO.

4. Elegant women are changing to REGAL

   TYPE   STATEMENT:

   POSSIBLE MEANING: SPOILT/TRENDY/IDLE RICH WOMEN ARE CHANGING TO REGAL.

   MY SIMILAR EXAMPLE: SMART KIDS ARE BUYING SKIDO BIKES.

5. Have your cat **put to sleep** gently at KITTIES.

   TYPE   STATEMENT:

   POSSIBLE MEANING: HAVE YOUR CAT KILLED AT KITTIES.

   MY SIMILAR EXAMPLE: THE AIR IS DIFFERENT AT STOCKYARD ACRES

6. See the **newest gear** in town at MYER'S.

   TYPE   STATEMENT:

   POSSIBLE MEANING: SEE SOME GEAR THAT WON'T SELL INTERSTATE/OR IN SOME OTHER CITY.

   MY SIMILAR EXAMPLE: FLY AWAY ON A MAGIC CARPET WITH EL CHEAPO AIRLINES.

INTEGRATING SKILLS

Exercises 34 aims to help you summarize information efficiently.

Summarizing involves shortening information and picking out the important ideas in it.

Summarizing involves thinking because you have to think about the following things in what you have read.

1. What is the MAIN IDEA or TOPIC being discussed?

2. Which sentence is the KEY SENTENCE? This tells you what the main topic or idea is.

3. Which sentences are NOT IMPORTANT? These sentences don't tell you much about the main topic. They usually refer to very specific or irrelevant details about the main topic or some other topic.

4. Which terms can be used instead of a list of related things or actions? For example **animals** instead of dogs, horses, cats, cows, and pigs, or, **she went to the movies** instead of she bought a ticket, sat in the back row, went to sleep in the movie, and caught a bus home.

READ EACH OF THE FOLLOWING BRIEF READINGS THROUGH ONCE TO GET AN IDEA OF WHAT EACH IS ABOUT. NOW AT THE END OF EACH SENTENCE MARK IN A

*   TO INDICATE THIS SENTENCE IS THE KEY SENTENCE.

X   TO INDICATE THIS SENTENCE IS UNIMPORTANT FOR A SUMMARY.

✓   TO INDICATE THIS SENTENCE IS USEFUL AND HELPS EXPLAIN THE MAIN IDEA OR TOPIC.

FINALLY, WRITE A SUMMARY OF THE READING IN **NO MORE** THAN 40 WORDS. GIVE YOUR SUMMARY A HEADING.

EXAMPLE

X { The men who built our nation looked on the wilderness they encountered as a repository of raw materials, land, and wealth. }

X { Colonists, pioneers, loggers, miners, railroaders, and captains of industry drew from it to fashion the wealthiest and most powerful nation on earth. }

✓ { But by so doing, they almost destroyed the very thing that had nurtured us. }

✓ { Whole forests were felled to build cities and undergird railroads, marshes were drained, swift-running rivers were silenced by dams. }

✓ { Today lonely beaches where spoonbills once nested sprout condominiums. The desert night blazes with the garish neon of cities. }

✓ { On western hills and northern lakes, the cries of coyotes and loons give way to the snort of road-building and industrial machines. }

* { Fortunately we Americans have come to a new awareness of the value of wilderness to our spiritual and physical well-being. }

✓ { And with passage of the Wilderness Act in 1964, we began to preserve much of what remains. }

X { A few years ago I flew to a remote lake }

×{ hidden in the folds of Alaska's forested mountains. Living in a small cabin, chopping my
×{ own firewood, relishing the pure air and the silence of wilderness nights, I felt the awaken-
×∫ ing of senses dulled by urban living. How much civilization has given us, I mused, but }×
how much we have lost!

John Muir had it right: "Climb the mountains and get their good tidings. Nature's }×

From: *National Geograhic*, Feb. 1974, Vol. 145, No. 2.

TITLE: SAVING AMERICA'S WILDERNESS

SUMMARY: (40 WORDS MAXIMUM):

AMERICANS ARE AT LAST AWARE OF HOW IMPORTANT THEIR WILDERNESS IS TO THEM. PIONEERS CUT FORESTS, DUG MINES AND DAMMED RIVERS WITHOUT THINKING OF THE DAMAGE TO THE WILDERNESS. MODERN AMERICANS HAVE ALSO CAUSED DAMAGE WITH BUILDINGS AND ROADS.

1.

It was an unlikely fishing party, for we sought a catch too small to see. }×

All three of us—two Fordham University students and I—were dressed for polar weather. Loading our toboggan at the edge }×
of an ice-covered lake near Armonk, New York, 30 miles north of Manhattan, we dragged it to a point about 150 yards offshore. ×

Half an hour later, in the comfortable warmth of a lakeside laboratory, I peered into a microscope at a drop of water to see what we had caught. There, magnified 1,000 times, danced and jostled bright green *Chlamydomonas,* lively micro-organisms, each with two }×
long, swishing "tails" called flagella.

They were algae—among the most widespread of living things, and among the hardiest. Algae grow in the perpetual ice and snow of polar regions, in near-boiling hot springs, and in brine lakes ten times saltier than the }√

sea. They even live in deserts, where they can survive indefinitely on traces of dew and spring into new growth when raindrops fall. }×

Algae. The word often evokes a sniff of distaste. This is the stuff that thrives on pollutants in our lakes and rivers, and reeks to }×
high heaven on a hot summer day. }√

But consider this. Without algae, it is ⸰
doubtful that man could have evolved and survived. Indeed, many biologists believe that
one-celled algae may have been the remote X
ancestors of all multicellular organisms. Perhaps as much as 90 percent of all photosynthesis is accomplished by algae. And in the }√
sea, as the vegetable part of plankton, they are the food upon which all life depends. }

There are about 30,000 species of algae, ranging from tiny one-celled organisms to such }√
seaweeds as giant kelp, which grows }

From: *National Geographic,* March 1974, p. 361.

TITLE: WE NEED ALGAE TO SURVIVE

SUMMARY: (40 WORDS MAXIMUM):

WE NEED ALGAE FOR HUMANS TO SURVIVE. MOST OF THE OXYGEN OF THE AIR IS MADE BY ALGAE. MOST SEA LIFE FEEDS ON ALGAE IN SOME WAY. ALGAE GROWS IN ALL TEMPERATURES. THERE ARE THOUSANDS OF DIFFERENT SPECIES OF ALGAE.

2.

x { Their shining surfaces are the playgrounds of millions of people; their dim bottoms are the resting-places of thousands of wrecks.

✓ { Benignly they serve two nations in many ways—cooling cities, quenching thirsts, carrying away sewage, generating electricity, fending off tornadoes, providing ocean ports a thousand miles inland.

x { Sometimes, in a less benign mood, they remind us that they were not placed on earth to be man's servants. With eroding waves, they

x { devour beaches and summer cottages. In the winter they batter with fists of ice at the works that man has built to control them.

x { Not idly are they called Great Lakes. After touring them from Minnesota wilderness to New York shores, I am astonished at how well man has managed to tame these

✱ watery gaints. But I am sobered by the injury he has inflicted and by the urgent task that he now faces in keeping the lakes alive. ✱

✓ } The Great Lakes cover nearly 25,000 square miles of North America, making them the greatest expanse of freshwater on this planet.

x } Even the smallest of them, Lake Ontario, ranks a respectable fourteenth among the world's largest lakes. Erie, Michigan, and Huran rank twelfth, sixth, and fifth. Lake Superior? Its area is second only to the salty Caspian Sea, which is also a lake by definition—being completely surrounded by land.

✓ } Slow to react to winter's chill and summer's heat, the Great Lakes play an important role as weather makers. When spring comes—tornado season in the Midwest—the lakes appear to exert a calming influence on the air that passes over them. The lakeside city of Grand

FROM: *National Geographic,* August 1973, p. 147-150

TITLE: ARE WE KILLING THE GREAT LAKES?

SUMMARY: (40 WORDS MAXIMUM):

HUMAN BEINGS HAVE BEEN INJURING THE GREAT LAKE FOR YEARS BY POLLUTING THEM. THEY ARE THE GREATEST EXPANSE OF FRESH WATER ON THIS PLANET. WE NEED THEM FOR COOLING CITIES, INLAND WATER, TRANSPORT AND FOR CONTROLLING THE WEATHER.

3.

X { Not since the depression of the 1930's had the economies of nations around the world suffered such peacetime disruption and strain.
X { Factories shut down, workers laid off, lights dimmed, buildings chilled, gasoline stations closed, Sunday driving was banned, fuel prices soared, stock markets fell, and shortages threatened in a host of products, from perfume to fertilizer.

✓ { Oil. For more than half a century it had been an inexpensive resource, a black milk of the earth on which nations fed and grew strong. The supply seemed infinite, and by 1973 this amazingly versatile substance had pervaded almost every phase of our lives.

X { Then the Arabs constricted the flow, with convulsive results. Saudi Arabia, largest oil producer in the Middle East, has a population less than 4 percent that of the United States and a gross national product scarcely one percent as large. Yet oil had become a

resource so vital that the most powerful industrial nations faced recession or, as in the case of Japan, outright collapse if Arab cutbacks persisted. ✓

Moreover, the United States awoke to the realization that the oil industry itself had grown so huge and so complex that few people could comprehend its operation. The combined assets of this nation's oil companies total more than 70 billion dollars. A number of these corporate giants operate with budgets exceeding those of many nations. X

I recently traveled nearly 50,000 miles in a globe-girdling journey that took me to 11 nations. Producers, consumers, businessmen, government officials, oil-field roughnecks, geologists—I talked to a host of people until the picture of a troubled industry took form. X

The shortage plaguing the United States, I discovered, was long in the making. ✱

From: *National Geographic,* June 1974, p. 792

TITLE: WORLD'S OIL SUPPLY RUNNING OUT

SUMMARY: (40 WORDS MAXIMUM):

THE WORLD'S OIL SUPPLY IS RAPIDLY RUNNING OUT. ALL COUNTRIES DEPEND ON OIL FOR TRANSPORT, JOBS AND PRODUCTS MADE FROM OIL. WITHOUT OIL NATIONS WOULD SUDDENLY FACE RECESSION AND COLLAPSE OF THEIR ECONOMY.

Do you have an idea to share?

We are always looking for quality manuscripts and video ideas that will be of benefit to others in the field. If you or one of your colleagues have a new, innovative, or effective approach to addressing timely issues, curriculum development, educator professionalism, or teaching, let us know. We'd like to hear from you. Contact:

Nancy Shin
Director of Publications

NEED MORE COPIES?

Need more copies of this book? Want your own copy? If so, you can order additional copies of *Teaching Students to Think* by using this form or by calling us TOLL FREE at 1-800-733-6786.

We guarantee complete satisfaction with all of our materials. If you are not completely satisfied with any NES publication, you may return it to us within 60 days for a full refund.

	Quantity	Total Price
Teaching Students to Think ($21.95 each)		
	_____	_____

Quantity discounts: 20-45 copies--save 15%
46-99 copies--save 35%
100+ copies--save 50%

Shipping:

Add $1.50 per copy
(There is no shipping charge when
you include payment with your order.)   _____

Indiana residents add 5% sales tax   _____

TOTAL   _____

Check enclosed with order   Please bill me

SHIP TO:

Name: _____ Title: _____

Organization: _____ Purchase Order No. _____

Address: _____

City/State/Zip: _____

Phone Number: _____

MAIL TO:

National Educational Service
1821 W. Third Street
P.O. Box 8
Bloomington, IN 47402

Teaching Students to Think is one of many publications produced by the National Educational Service. Our mission is to provide you and other leaders in education, business, and government with top-quality publications, videos, and conferences. If you have any questions or comments about *Teaching Students to Think* or any of our other publications or services, please contact us at:

National Educational Service
1821 W. Third St., Suite 201
P.O. Box 8
Bloomington, IN 47402
(812) 336-7700